I0061578

Miller Christy

The Trade Signs of Essex

Miller Christy

The Trade Signs of Essex

ISBN/EAN: 9783744675772

Printed in Europe, USA, Canada, Australia, Japan

Cover: Foto ©ninafisch / pixelio.de

More available books at **www.hansebooks.com**

THE

▓RADE ▓IGNS OF ▓SSEX:

A Popular Account

OF

THE ORIGIN AND MEANINGS

OF THE

Public House & Other Signs

NOW OR FORMERLY

Found in the County of Essex.

BY

MILLER CHRISTY,

Author of " Manitoba Described," " The Genus Primula in Essex," "Our Empire," &c.

WITH ILLUSTRATIONS.

Chelmsford :

EDMUND DURRANT & Co., 90, HIGH STREET.

London :

GRIFFITH, FARRAN, OKEDEN, AND WELSH,

WEST CORNER ST. PAUL'S CHURCHYARD.

—

MDCCCLXXXVII.

PREFACE.

——:o:——

" Prefaces to books [says a learned author] are like signs to public-houses. They are intended to give one an idea of the kind of entertainment to be found within."

STUDENT of the ancient and peculiarly interesting Art of Heraldry can hardly fail, at an early period in his researches, to be struck with the idea that some connection obviously exists between the various "charges," "crests," "badges," and "supporters" with which he is familiar, and the curious designs now to be seen upon the sign-boards of many of our roadside inns, and which were formerly displayed by most other houses of business.

On first noticing this relationship when commencing the study of Heraldry, somewhere about the year 1879, it occurred to me that the subject was well worth following up. It seemed to me that much interesting information would probably be brought to light by a careful examination of the numerous signs of my native county of Essex. Still more desirable did this appear when, after careful inquiry, I found that (so far as I was able to discover) no more than three systematic treatises upon the subject had ever been published. First and foremost among these stands Messrs. Larwood and Hotten's *History of Sign-boards*,[1] a standard work which is

---

[1] *The History of Sign-boards, From the Earliest Times to the Present Day.* By Jacob Larwood and John Camden Hotten. London, 1867. In this otherwise excellent work there is, unfortunately, no connection between the illustrations and the letterpress.

evidently the result of a very large amount of labour and research. I do not wish to conceal the extent to which I am indebted to it. It is, however, to be regretted that the authors should have paid so much attention to London signs, to the partial neglect of those in other parts of the country, and that they should not have provided a more complete index; but it is significant of the completeness of their work that the other two writers upon the subject have been able to add very little that is new, beside mere local details. A second dissertation upon the origin and use of trade-signs is to be found in a most interesting series of articles upon the signs of the Town of Derby, contributed to the *Reliquary*[1] in 1867 by the late Mr. Llewellyn Jewitt, F.S.A., the editor of that magazine; while the third and last source of information is to be found in a lengthy pamphlet by Mr. Wm. Pengelly, F.R.S., treating in detail of the Devonshire signs.[2]

On the Continent the literature of signs is much more voluminous. Among the chief works may be mentioned Mons. J. D. Blavignac's *Histoire des Enseignes d'Hôtelleries, d'Auberges, et de Cabarets;*[3] Mons. Edouard Fournier's *Histoire des Enseignes de Paris;*[4] and Mons. Eustache de La Quérière's *Recherches Historiques sur les Enseignes des Maisons Particulières.*[5]

It should be pointed out here that, although in what follows a good deal has been said as to the age and past history of many of the best-known Essex inns, this is, strictly speaking, a treatise on Signs and Sign-boards only. The two subjects are, however, so closely connected that I have found it best to treat them as one.

There will, doubtless, be many who will say that much of what I have hereafter advanced is of too speculative a nature to be of real value. They will declare, too, that I have

[1] Vol. viii. No. 27, p. 175 *et seq.*
[2] Reprinted in 1872 from the *Transactions of the Devonshire Association for the Advancement of Literature, Science, and Art.* 93 pp. 8vo.
[3] Geneva: Grosset et Trembley, 1878, 8vo, 542 pp.
[4] Edited by le Bibliophile Jacob, with appendix, frontispiece, 84 wood-engravings, and a Map of Paris in the Fifteenth Century. Paris: E. Dentu, 1884.
[5] Paris and Rouen, 1852, 8vo, 131 pp.

shown far too great a readiness to ascribe to an heraldic origin, signs which are at least as likely to have been derived from some other source. To these objections I may fairly reply that as, in most cases, no means now exist of discovering the precise mode of origination, centuries ago, of many of our modern signs, it is impossible to do much more than speculate as to their derivation; and the fact that it has been found possible to ascribe such large numbers to a probable heraldic origin affords, to my thinking, all the excuse that is needed for so many attempts having been made to show that others have been derived from the same source.

No one is more fully aware than I am of the incompleteness of my work. Many very interesting facts relating to Essex inns and their signs have unquestionably been omitted. But the search after all such facts is practically an endless one. If, for instance, I had been able to state the history of all the inns and their signs in every town and village in the county with the completeness with which (thanks to Mr. H. W. King) I have been enabled to treat those of Leigh, I should have swelled my book to encyclopædic dimensions, and should have had to ask for it a prohibitory price.

In a treatise involving such an immense amount of minute detail, it is impossible to avoid some errors. My hope is, however, that these are not many. I shall always be glad to have pointed out to me any oversights which may be detected, and I shall be not less glad at all times to receive any additional facts which my readers may be kind enough to send me.

I regret that it has been necessary to make use of some old heraldic terms which the general reader will probably not at first understand. This, however, was quite unavoidable. The meaning of these terms will be at once made clear on reference to the Glossary given at the end of the work, as an Appendix.

According to the list given in the last edition of the *Essex Post Office Directory* there are now existing in the county no less than one thousand, three hundred and fifty-five inns and public-houses. The signs of all these have been classified, arranged under various headings, and treated of in turn, to-

gether with a very large number of others which have existed
in the county during the last two centuries and a half, but
have now disappeared. Information as to these has been
collected by means of a careful examination of the trade-
tokens of the seventeenth century, old Essex Directories,
early books and pamphlets relating to the county, old deeds
and records, the early issues of the *Chelmsford Chronicle*
(now the *Essex County Chronicle*), and other newspapers,
&c., &c. Altogether it will be found I have been able to
enumerate no less than 693 distinct signs as now or formerly
occurring in Essex.

I am indebted to a large number of gentlemen who have
most kindly assisted me by supplying me with information,
suggestions, &c., during the eight years I have been gathering
material for the present book. First and foremost among
these I must mention Mr. H. W. King of Leigh, Hon. Secretary to the Essex Archæological Society, who, as he says,
"knows the descent of nearly every house and plot of ground
in the parish for two or three generations, and the name of
every owner." Among other gentlemen to whom I am indebted in varying degrees, I may mention Mr. G. F. Beaumont, Mr. Fred. Chancellor, that veteran Essex archæologist
Mr. Joseph Clarke, F.S.A., Mr. Wm. Cole, F.E.S., Hon.
Secretary of the Essex Field Club, Mr. Thos. B. Daniell,
the Rev. H. L. Elliot, Mr. C. K. Probert, Mr. G. N. Maynard, Mr. H. Ecroyd Smith, and others, I have also to
express my thanks to the following gentlemen, magistrates'
clerks to the various Petty Sessional Divisions of Essex,
who have most kindly supplied me with lists of such beer-
houses as have signs in their respective divisions :—Messrs.
A. J. Arthy (Rochford), Jos. Beaumont (Dengie), W. Bin-
don Blood (Witham), J. and J. T. Collin (Saffron Walden),
G. Creed (Epping and Harlow), Augustus Cunnington
(Freshwell and South Hinckford), W. W. Duffield (Chelmsford), H. S. Haynes (Havering), A. H. Hunt (Orsett), and
Chas. Smith (Ongar). I have also to thank the Essex
Archæological Society for the use of the four blocks of the
De Vere badges appearing on p. 70 ; the Essex Field Club

for that of the Rose Inn, Peldon, on p. 118; Messrs. Chambers & Sons of 22, Wilson Street, Finsbury, for that of the Brewers' Arms on p. 32; Messrs. Couchman & Co. of 14, Throgmorton Street, E.C., for that of the Drapers' Arms on p. 40; and the Brewers', Drapers' and Butchers' Companies for kindly allowing me to insert cuts of their arms. To my cousin, Miss S. Christy, I am indebted for kindly drawing the illustrations appearing on pp. 87 and 140.

Portions of the Introduction and other parts of the book have already appeared in an altered form in *Chambers's Journal* (Jan., 1887, p. 785), and I am indebted to the editor for permission to reprint.

Finally, I have to thank the Subscribers, who, by kindly ordering copies, have diminished the loss which almost invariably attends the publication of works of this nature. As the book has already extended to considerably more space than was originally intended, I trust the Subscribers will excuse the omission of the customary list.

Miller Christy

CHELMSFORD,
    February 1, 1887.

CONTENTS.

——:o:——

CONTENTS.

The Trade Signs of Essex.

CHAPTER I.

INTRODUCTION.

"The county god, ...
  Whose blazing wyvern weather-cocked the spire,
  Stood from his walls, and winged his entry-gates,
  And swang besides on many a windy sign."
                    TENNYSON : *Aylmer's Field.*

THE use of signs as a means of distinguishing different houses of business, is a custom which has come down to us from times of great antiquity. Nevertheless, it is not at all difficult to discover the reasons which first led to their being employed. In days when only an infinitesimally small proportion of the population could read, it would obviously have been absurd for a tradesman to have inscribed above his door his name and occupation, or the number of his house, as is now done. Such inscriptions as "Sutton & Sons, Seedsmen," or " Pears & Co., Soapmakers," would then have been quite useless as a means of distinguishing the particular houses that bore them ; but, if each dealer displayed conspicuously before his place of business a painted representation of the wares he sold, the arms of the Trade-Guild to which he belonged, or those of his landlord or patron, or some other device by which his house might be known, there would be little probability of mistake. If the sign thus displayed indicated the nature of the wares sold within, it would answer a double purpose. Signs, too, would be especially

2

useful in distinguishing different establishments in times when many members of the same craft resided, as they used formerly to do, in one street or district. Although this habit has now largely disappeared in England, in the cities of the East each trade is still chiefly confined to its own special quarter.

In considering the subject of how signs originally came into use, it must never be forgotten that, in bygone times, they were not confined, as now, almost exclusively to " public-houses." We have still, among others, the sign of the POLE for a barber, the ROD AND FISH for a tackle-dealer, the BLACK BOY for a tobacconist, the GOLDEN BALLS for a pawn-broker ; but formerly the proprietor of nearly every house of business, and even of private residences, displayed his own particular sign, just as the keepers of inns and taverns do now. For instance, an examination of the title-page of almost any book, published a couple of centuries or so ago, will show an imprint something like the following:— " Printed for Timothy Childe at the WHITE HART in St. Paul's Churchyard ; and for Thos. Varnam and John Osborn at the OXFORD ARMS in Lombard St. MDCCXII." Again, Sir Richard Baker's quaint *Chronicles of the Kings of England* was printed in 1684, " for H. Sawbridge at the BIBLE on Ludgate Hill, B. Tooke at the SHIP in St. Paul's Church-yard, and T. Sawbridge at the THREE FLOWER-DE-LUCES in Little Brittain." As a further example of the use of signs in former times by booksellers, in common with other trades-men, it may be mentioned that, according to a writer in *Frazer's Magazine* (1845, vol. xxxii. p. 676)—

"The first edition of Shakespeare's *Venus and Adonis,* and the first edition of his *Rape of Lucrece,* were ' sold by John Harrison at the sign of the WHITE GREYHOUND in Saint Paul's Churchyard ; ' and the first edition of *Shepheard's Kalender* by ' Hugh Singleton, dwelling at the GOLDEN TUN, in Creed Lane, near unto Ludgate.' The first edition of *The Merry Wives of Windsor* was sold at the FLOWER DE LEUSE AND CROWNE in St. Paul's Churchyard ; the first edition of the *Midsummer Night's Dream* at the WHITE HART in Fleet Street ; the first edition of the *Merchant of Venice* at the GREEN DRAGON in St. Paul's Churchyard ; the first edition of *Richard III.* at the ANGEL, and the first edition of *Richard II.* at the FOX, both in St. Paul's Churchyard ; the first edition of *Henry V.* was sold at the CAT AND PARROTS in Cornhill ; the first edition of *Lear* at the PIED BULL in St. Paul's Churchyard; and the first edition of *Othello* 'at the EAGLE AND CHILD in Britain's Bourse'—*i.e.*, the New Exchange."

Were announcements similar to these to appear on any modern book, it would certainly give many persons the impression that the work had been printed at a "public-house." Again, on the cheques, and over the door of Messrs. Hoare, bankers, of Fleet Street, may still be seen a representation of the LEATHER BOTTLE which formed their sign in Cheapside at least as long ago as the year 1677. In Paris, to the present day, sellers of "*bois et charbons*" (wood and charcoal or coals) invariably have the fronts of their establishments, facing the street, painted in a manner intended to convey the impression that the house is built of rough logs of wood. This device, although not displayed upon a sign-board, forms, in every respect, a true trade-sign. In all parts of France, signs still retain much more of their ancient glory than they do in England. Though not common in the newer and more fashionable streets and boulevards, they are abundant in the older quarters of Paris, Rouen, and other large towns. They are much oftener pictorial or graven than with us, and it is notable that they are used almost, or quite, as frequently by shopkeepers and other tradesmen as by the keepers of wine-shops, inns, and taverns. The sign, too, very often represents the wares sold within.

Nowadays, however, the old custom of displaying a sign finds favour with very few English tradesmen, except the keepers of inns and taverns; and even they have allowed the custom to sink to such depths of degradation that the great majority of sign-boards now bear only the name of the house in print: consequently the reason which led originally to the use of signs—the necessity for pictorial representation when few could read—is no longer obvious. It may be truly said that the great spread of education among all classes during the present century has given a death-blow alike to the use of signs in trade and to the art of the sign-painter. This, to be sure, is hardly a matter to call for regret on its own account. Nevertheless, the great decline in the use of the old-fashioned pictorial sign-board is to be regretted for many reasons. The signs which our forefathers made use of have interwoven themselves with our whole domestic, and even, to some extent, with our political, history. In losing them we are losing one of the well-known landmarks of the past. Sign-boards of the real old sort have about them an amount of interest which is sufficient to surprise those who care to take trouble in studying them. Dr. Brewer very truly says, in his *Dictionary of Phrase and Fable* :—"Much of a nation's history, and more of its manners and feelings, may be gleaned from its public-house signs." The sign-boards themselves tell us (as has already been pointed out) of the habit our forefathers had of crowding together in one street or district all those who were of a like occupation or profession. They tell us also of the deep ignorance of the masses of the people in days when sign-boards were a necessity. And when it is remembered that it was only so lately as the beginning of the present century that the knowledge of reading and writing became sufficiently widespread to allow the numbering of houses to come into general use as a means of distinguishing one house from another, it will be easily seen that the sign-boards of (say) two centuries ago played a very important, and even an essential, part in the commercial world of those days.

But a study of the various devices that appear even on modern sign-boards will teach us still more of the doings of our ancestors. They tell us of the wares our forefathers made and dealt in, of the superstitious beliefs they held, of the party strifes in which they engaged, and of the great titled families which had so large a share in the making of English history—in short, the devices seen, even on modern sign-boards, afford, to those who can and care to read them, no mean picture both of mediæval and more modern times. It was well remarked in an early number of the *Gentleman's Magazine* (1738, vol. viii. p. 526), that "The People of England are a nation of Politicians, from the First Minister down to the cobbler, and peculiarly remarkable for hanging out their principles upon their sign-posts." Some of our

modern Essex signs, for instance, are relics (as will be more
clearly pointed out hereafter) of what were once staple industries in the county, though now all but unknown in it. Thus
the signs of the WOOLPACK (p. 79), the SHEARS (p. 41), and
the GOLDEN FLEECE (p. 78) are all mementoes of the time
when the woollen trade flourished in Essex. The sign of
the HOP-POLES (p. 111) reminds us of the time when hop-
growing formed a considerable industry in the county. Our
various BLUE BOARS (p. 68) speak to us of the noble and
once mighty Essex family of De Vere, which formerly
wielded a great power in England. These are but a few
instances. Others will occur to every one who peruses the
following pages. At the present day, too, there is scarcely a
village in the county that has not some street, square, or
lane named after an inn-sign, as, for instance, Sun Street,
Eagle Lane, Swan Street, Falcon Square, Lion Walk,
Greyhound Lane, &c. In London, or Paris, the connection
is still closer. Surely, then, although signs are no longer of
great or urgent importance to us in the daily routine of our
ordinary business life, an inquiry into their past history will
be a matter of much interest, especially as comparatively
little has hitherto been written about them.

Nevertheless, although it is certain that (as has been
stated) not a few of our present signs have been derived from
emblems of industries now decayed and the armorial bearings
of ancient county families, the fact cannot be overlooked that
in a great many cases these particular signs, as now displayed
by particular houses, have only very recently come into use.
That is to say, they are only *indirectly* derived from the
sources named, having been selected because, perhaps, some
neighbouring and really ancient inn (which derived its sign
directly) was known to have long borne that sign. There
can be no doubt (as Mr. H. W. King writes) that—

" The very large majority of country inns are comparatively modern, both
as to signs and sites. Elsewhere, as here [Leigh], I suspect they have
been moved and removed again and again—old signs shifted, and often
changed altogether. I remember the late Mr. Edward Woodard, of
Billericay, telling me some years ago that the inns of that town had been
changed again and again : that is, what are now private residences were

formerly inns, and *vice versa*. This he knew from the evidence of con-
veyances which had passed through his hands professionally. I have no
doubt that every town would show the same facts if only one could get
sufficient evidence. At the same time, of course, some inns are very old
indeed, both as to sites and signs."

The great decay in the use of inn-signs of the real old sort
has, it is much to be feared, now gone too far to be arrested,
however much it may be regretted. In Essex, probably not
five per cent. of our sign-boards are now pictorial. Even in
the remote and sleepy little town of Thaxted very few of the
inns now possess pictorial signs. Here and there, however,
throughout the county one may still come across a few
such, and several excellent examples will be hereafter
alluded to.

Probably no better idea can now be obtained in Essex of an
old-fashioned thoroughfare than in the broad High Street at
Epping. From one point no less than ten sign-boards may
be seen, all swinging over the pavement in the ancient
style. Only one, however, the WHITE LION, is now pictorial.
The number of inns in Grays, too, is very large. It has been
stated in print that "for its size, it contains more than any
other town in England." In the narrow Tindal Street at
Chelmsford the sign-boards still swing across the street in
the old style, and are hung upon the old supports. The best
example is that which supports the sign of the SPOTTED
DOG. Witham has many inns, nearly all of which have
their sign-boards hanging over the pavement, but neither
they nor their supports are of much interest. Colchester
has hardly such a thing as a projecting sign-board, let alone
pictorial signs. Castle Hedingham, for its size, probably has
more pictorial signs than any other Essex town, the BELL,
the CROWN, the THREE CROWNS, and the RISING SUN being
all thus represented. Except the sign-iron of the SIX BELLS
(p. 168), Dunmow contains but little of sign-board interest.
The only pictorial sign-board in Ongar is that of the COCK.
Several signs and sign-irons in Bardfield are hereafter
noticed (pp. 170 and 169). In the High Street at Romford
are many very old inns, but their signs are all script.
At Leigh there are many inns, the most ancient of which,

in the opinion of Mr. H. W. King, are the CROWN and the
HAMBORO' MERCHANTS' ARMS, though the GEORGE was
originally the more important.

The following interesting list of inns in the Epping Division
in September, 1789, has been kindly contributed by Mr. G.
Creed of Epping :—

CHINGFORD : King's Head, Bull. EPPING : White Lion, Bell, Cock,
Swan, Black Lion, Epping Place, Cock and Magpie, Green Man, Globe,
George, Rose and Crown, Thatched House, White Hart, Harp, White
Horse, Sun, Chequers. NAZING : Chequer, Sun, Coach and Horses,
Crown, King Harold's Head. ROYDON : Fish and Eels, Black Swan,
New Inn, White Hart, Green Man. WALTHAM ABBEY : Owl, Green
Man, Harp, Greyhound, Ship, Cock, Chequer, Angel, Rose and Crown,
Red Lion, Bull's Head, Three Tons (*sic*), Sun, Cock, New Inn, Green
Dragon, White Horse, Compasses, White Lion, King's Arms. CHIG-
WELL : Three Jolly Wheelers, Roebuck, King's Head, Maypole, Bald
Hind, Fox and Hounds, Bald Stag. LOUGHTON : Reindeer, Crown,
King's Head, Plume of - Feathers. MORETON : Nag's Head, Green
Man, White Hart. NORTH WEALD : Rainbow, King's Head. STANFORD
RIVERS : White Bear, Green Man. THEYDON BOIS : White Hart.
THEYDON GARNON : Merry Fiddlers. GREAT HALLINGBURY : George.
LATTON : Sun and Whalebone, Bush Fair House. FYFIELD : Black
Bull, Queen's Head. LAMBOURNE : White Hart, Blue Boar. HIGH
LAVER : Chequer. LITTLE LAVER : Leather Bottle. MAGDALEN LAVER :
Green Man. CHIPPING ONGAR : White Horse, King's Head, Anchor,
Crown, Red Lion, Bull, Cock. HIGH ONGAR : Red Lion, White Horse,
Two Brewers. HARLOW : King's Head, Black Bull, George, Green
Man, White Horse, Horns and Horseshoes, Queen's Head, Black Lion,
Marquis of Granby. HATFIELD BROAD OAK : Plume of Feathers,
White Horse, Cock, Duke's Head, Bald-Faced Stag, Red Lion, Crown.
SHEERING : Crown, Cock. NETTESWELL : White Horse, Chequer. GREAT
PARNDON : Cock, Three Horse Shoes.

In the last edition of the *London Directory*, 82 firms are still
described as "sign-painters," and in the *Essex Directory*, 10 ;
but it is certain that most of these follow also some other
trade than sign-painting. In some cases artists of eminence
have been known to paint signs for inns, but there does not
appear to have been any notable instances of this in Essex.
As a rule our pictorial sign-boards are not works of art. That
this is a common failing elsewhere, is shown by the fact that
the French say of a bad portrait or picture, " qu'il n'est bon
qu'à faire une enseigne à bière." Signs, it must be admitted,
are among those things which the enlightenment of this go-
ahead nineteenth century is rapidly improving off the face of

the earth. Yet one cannot but agree with the writer in
Frazer's Magazine, already quoted, who aptly observes that
it is a thousand pities the old signs were ever taken down.
"Men might," he says, "read something of history (to say
nothing of a hash of heraldry) in their different devices."

This decay in the use of inn-signs, however, is no greater
than the decline in importance of the inns themselves. These
have within quite recent years fallen from a position of great
eminence and prosperity to one of comparative degradation.
Up to about fifty years ago, inns were the centres round
which most events of the time revolved. They combined
within themselves, to a very large extent, the various uses
to which modern clubs, reading-rooms, institutes, railway
stations, restaurants, eating-houses, hotels, public-houses,
livery-stables, and the like are now severally put. At present
the majority of our inns are little more than tippling-houses
or drinking-places for the poorer classes. The upper stratum
of society has but little connection with them, beyond re-
ceiving their rents.

Nothing has done more to promote this lowering of the
status of modern inns in general than the disuse of coaching.
Inns were the starting-points and destinations of the old
coaches, and travellers naturally put up and took their
meals at them. Now people travel by rail, stop at railway
stations, put up at the "Railway Hotel," and get their
meals in the station "refreshment rooms." In days, too,
when country inns formed the stopping-places of the coaches
they naturally became important centres of information. In
this they answered the purpose to which clubs, institutes,
reading-rooms, and the like are now put. The cheap newspapers of to-day have given another serious shock to the
old tavern life of last century. Then, too, the innumerable
horses, needed for the many coaches on the great high-roads
of fifty or a hundred years ago, were kept at the inns, to
the great advantage of the latter. Now the various railway
companies, of course, provide their own engines, and the
old-fashioned inns have to content themselves with a very
limited posting or omnibus business.

It is, indeed, not too much to say that in the old coaching days a small town or village on any main road often consisted largely or almost entirely of inns, and lived upon the traffic. Supplying the necessaries for this traffic may be said to have been "the local industry" by which the inhabitants of such places lived. Evidences of this may be gained from not a few old books. Thus in Ogilby's *Traveller's Guide*, a book of the roads published in 1699, Bow, near Stratford, is said to be "full of inns," while Stratford and Kelvedon are both spoken of as "consisting chiefly of inns." Again, in Daniel Defoe's *Tour through the whole Island of Great Britain*, published in 1724 (vol. i. p. 52), it is said that—

"Brent-Wood and Ingarstone, and even Chelmsford itself, have very little to be said of them, but that they are large thorough-fair Towns, full of good Inns, and chiefly maintained by the excessive Multitude of Carriers and Passengers, which are constantly passing this Way, with Droves of Cattle, Provisions, and Manufactures for London."

Few persons of the present day have any adequate idea of the extent to which tavern life influenced thought and manners seventy, eighty, or one hundred years ago. Each man then had his tavern, much as we now have our clubs and reading-rooms. There he met his friends every evening, discussed the political questions of the day, talked over business topics, and heard the expensive and highly-valued London newspapers read aloud. Dickens, in *Barnaby Rudge*, has well sketched the select village company, which, for forty or fifty years, had met nightly in the bar of the old MAYPOLE to tipple and debate. Ale was the universal beverage on these occasions, and the fame of any given tavern was great or small according to the skill of the landlord or his servants in producing this beverage. It was not then, as now, the product of colossal breweries at Burton, Romford, or elsewhere, but was entirely brewed upon the premises of those who retailed it. Such customs as these, however, are now almost entirely of the past.

We will now return once more to the discussion of signboards and their modern degeneration. When signs were in general use by all tradesmen, it was but natural that people should endeavour to outvie one another in the prominence and obtrusiveness of their sign-boards. Exactly the same thing may be seen at the present day on any hoarding which the bill-sticker has ornamented with his flaring posters. These are of all imaginable colours and designs, in order to advertise and draw attention to the wares of rival tradesmen, each of whom endeavours to obtain greater publicity and attract more attention than his neighbour. Many were the devices made use of a century or more ago to draw attention to the sign-boards of those times. Some of the boards were made of enormous size; others were painted in flaring colours; others bore striking or amusing devices, likely to be remembered by those who saw them; while others were projected far out into the street, or hung in elaborate and ornamental frameworks of iron. When each man endeavoured to outdo his neighbour in these particulars, it may well be imagined that no slight inconvenience was caused to the public. Complaints that the size and prominence of the sign-boards in the London streets prevented the access of sunlight and the free circulation of the air began to be heard, according to Messrs. Larwood and Hotten, as early as the beginning of the fifteenth century, and an order was made to do away with the nuisance. In the course of time, however, the evil grew again, till Charles II., in 1667, "ordered that in all the streets no sign-board shall hang across, but that the sign shall be fixed against the balconies, or some convenient part of the side of the house." Again, however, the nuisance grew, and in 1762 large powers were once more granted for clearing away the too obtrusive signboards, and very many were taken down.

In France and other continental countries the same evil has had to be grappled with. Time after time, as reference to the works previously mentioned will show, the police of Paris and other large towns have issued orders concerning the pulling down and putting up of sign-boards. All Parisian signs are, consequently, now fastened to the fronts of the houses.

This regulation of sign-boards is not altogether unknown, even at the present day, in England. In the *Sussex Daily News* as lately as last October there appeared an account of the removal of two sign-boards that had recently been erected in two of the principal streets of Brighton. These boards, measuring respectively 48 inches by 30, and 48 inches by 18, were swung over the pavement at the respective heights of 15 feet and 12 feet ; yet, although there are scores of more obstructive sign-boards and sun-blinds in the borough, the somewhat over-officious Works Committee of the Corporation ordered that they should be removed by the surveyor, and the cost of so doing recovered from their owners, because, in the opinion of the Committee, such boards were " public annoyances and nuisances, by reason of their projecting over the highways and annoying the public passage along the streets." Presumably it is within the power of any Local Authority to remove, or direct the alteration of, any sign-boards which it regards as " nuisances."

A writer, styling himself "Ambulator," in the *Gentleman's Magazine* (vol. xl. p. 403) observes, so long ago as the year 1770, that signs "were certainly the effect of a general want of literature, and therefore can no longer be thought necessary, without national disgrace." He adds, though he must be guilty of exaggeration, that " there is, at present, scarce a child among the poorest of the people who, at seven or eight years old, cannot read a man's name and trade upon his door or window-shutter ; and therefore we want the sign-painter no more." He also says that—

" Long after signs became unnecessary, it was not unusual for an opulent shopkeeper to lay out as much upon a sign, and the curious ironwork with which it was fixed to his house, so as to project nearly into the middle of the street, as would furnish a less considerable dealer with a stock-in-trade. I have been credibly informed that there were many signs and sign-irons upon Ludgate Hill which cost several hundred pounds, and that as much was laid out by a mercer upon a sign of the Queen's Head as would have gone a long way towards decorating the original for a birth-night."

A good idea of how our Essex streets were obstructed by the huge dimensions of the signs of the various inns a century or more ago, may be obtained from an old print engraved by J. Ryland in 1762. It shows a view of the High Street of Chelmsford, taken from the point at which the fountain opposite the end of Springfield Lane now stands, and is entitled *A Perspective View of the County Town of Chelmsford, in Essex, with the Judge's Procession on the Day of Entrance, attended by the High Sheriff and his Officers.* The judge's carriage, drawn by six horses and preceded by the old " javelin men,"now dispensed with, is shown in its progress up the street, past the old BLACK BOY Inn, and going towards the church. The procession is passing under the great beam from which swings the sign of the BLACK BOY. This beam extends out from the house to the top of a post set up in the middle of the street for its support. If the height of this post may be estimated from the height of two persons shown standing near its base (who may be fairly set down as six feet in stature), it is not less than 28 feet high, while the beam it supports must project at least 33 feet from the house. Close to this structure, but nearer the other side of the street, though still not far from its middle, stands another sign-post of even more gigantic proportions. This post is very massive, and (if its height may be estimated in the same manner as before) it must be at least 24 feet high. Against the substantial shores supporting it in its upright position, leans a fiddler; while, close at hand, two mounted trumpeters are saluting the passing judge. But this is not all : upon the top of the post, supported by a fine iron framework, of an excellent flowing design, is the sign-board. This displays a *lion rampant guardant* (as the heralds say), which is evidently the sign of the large inn opposite to which it stands. This brings the height of the entire structure up to at least 45 feet, or nearly as high as the inn itself. This was probably the sign of the ancient LION Inn mentioned hereafter (p. 59).

Mr. F. T. Veley of Chelmsford possesses a fine old oil painting from which this engraving was evidently made, though the two differ in some particulars. The figures and the houses are almost precisely alike in both, but the painting has not the signs and sign-posts shown in the engraving. In both the width of the street is much too great. The engraving has been reduced by the photographic process, and is herein made use of as a frontispiece,[1] whilst the design of the remarkably fine iron framework supporting the sign of the LION has been reproduced upon the cover of the book. It is a remarkable fine example of the elaborate and ornamental sign-iron within which swung many sign-boards of a hundred years ago. Other examples, but less elegant, still remain here and there in the county, generally much rusted with age. Among these may be mentioned those of the SIX BELLS at Dunmow, which is dated 1778 (p. 168), the BELL at Bardfield (p. 170), and the BELL at Castle Hedingham (p. 150), all of which will be found depicted hereafter, though with other signs attached.

Leaving now the consideration of the *origin of the use of signs,* in order to discuss the *origins of the various devices used as signs,* we may well feel some surprise at first that the ancient and extremely entertaining, though now much decayed, art of Heraldry should have given us, at the present day, so many of our commonest signs as it obviously has done. A somewhat hasty examination of the list of Essex signs will show that something like 40 per cent. of the whole have probably been derived, either directly or indirectly, from Heraldry. The same statement would probably be found to hold good of the rest of England. So obvious is it that a very large number of inn-signs have been in some way derived from Heraldry, that it is surprising this connection has not received a much fuller recognition in the past than it has done. It is impossible, even for those most strongly inclined to disbelieve in the heraldic origin of a majority of our signs, to deny that very many of them, at least, have been so derived. Allusion is here made to such signs as the GRIFFIN, the BLUE BOAR, the GREEN DRAGON, the BLUE LION, the RED LION, the THREE CROWNS, the WHITE HART, the FLEUR-DE-LYS, the ROSE AND CROWN, the CROSS KEYS, and many others, the difficulty of ascribing which to any

[1] India proofs have also been struck off, and may be obtained separately, price 1s., from Messrs. Edm. Durrant & Co., Chelmsford.

other than an heraldic origin will be at once apparent. Indeed, the fact that a very large proportion of our signs are of
an heraldic derivation seems to require no stronger proof than
will be found in the following pages.   The next thing, therefore, will be to show how this came about.

It would probably early have suggested itself to the minds
of tradesmen and others to use their own coats of arms (when
they had any), or those of the Trade Guilds to which they
belonged, or the arms, crest, or badge[1] of their landlord or
some patron, as a sign.   This convenient custom, once
established, would be sure to be largely followed.   There
can be no doubt whatever that in this way arose the custom
of calling a house the " So-and-So's Arms."   At the present
time, the custom itself remains, although its origin has been
largely lost sight of ; and many inns have now, in consequence, come to be known as the " Arms " of persons, trades,
places, and things which never did bear, and never could have
borne, a coat of arms.   Clearly the origin of the sign of the
KING'S ARMS had never presented itself to the mind of the
" simple clodhopper " who, according to Messrs. Larwood and
Hotten (p. 106), " once walked many miles to see King George
IV. on one of his journeys, and came home mightily dis-
gusted ; for the king had arms just like any other man, while
he had always understood that his Majesty's right arm was
a lion, and his left a unicorn ! "   In Essex no less than 8·5
per cent. of all the inn-signs are " Arms " of some kind.   In
Devonshire " Arms " actually form as much as 22 per cent.
of the whole, according to Mr. Pengelly.

Although the custom of calling a house the " Somebody's
Arms " still survives, it is probable that, when the knowledge
and ordinary use of Heraldry began to decline, many houses,
formerly known as the " So-and-So's Arms," gradually came
to be called after the most prominent charge in the coat, or
after the " crest " or one of the " supporters,"[2] which might

---

[1] For an explanation of this, and all other heraldic terms hereafter, see
the Glossary of such terms, given as an Appendix, at the end.

[2] " Supporters," as explained in the Glossary at the end, are the animals
represented as holding up or *supporting* the shields of arms of royal and
other distinguished personages.   They are referred to in an amusing

have been a *lion gules*, a *boar azure*, a *white hart*, or a *rose crowned*. The badge, again, has unquestionably given us not a few signs. Badges were used by the sovereign and by the higher nobility from the fourteenth to the sixteenth centuries inclusive. They must not be confounded with *crests*, which were personal emblems, worn on the crest or helm by leaders in the field. *Badges*, on the other hand, were household emblems, worn by all the followers and retainers of the lord. They were always of a simple nature, to be easily distinguishable in battle, and were placed on armour, standards, clothing, buildings, furniture, &c., &c. As a rule, therefore, it is the badge, rather than the crest, or even the coat of arms, which has given us our old heraldic signs. In some cases badges were adopted by parties, as, for instance, during the Wars of the Roses, so called because the Yorkists took the White Rose as their badge, while the Lancastrians took the Red. Shakespeare often alludes to the old custom of using badges. Mrs. Bury Palliser,[1] speaking of this subject, says, that " we still find the cognizance of many an illustrious family preserved as the sign of an inn. The White Hart of Richard II., the Antelope of Henry IV., the Beacon of Henry V., the Feathers of Henry VI., the Star of the Lords of Oxford (whose brilliancy decided the fate of the Battle of Barnet), the Lion of the Duke of Norfolk (which shone conspicuous on Bosworth field), and many others, too numerous to mention, may yet be seen as sign-boards to village inns contiguous to the former castles of families whose possessions have passed into other hands." From the red shield (*roth schild*), above the door of the house of an honest old Hebrew, forming No. 148 in the *Juden Gasse*, or Jews' Alley, at Frankfort, has been derived the name of the richest family in the world.

From these heraldic devices have unquestionably been derived many of the strangely-coloured animals, such as red and

manner by the inimitably comic Dickens, who, in *Little Dorrit*, puts into the mouth of his by no means pleasant character, Flora Finch, the description of them quoted at the head of the following chapter.
[1] *Historic Devices, Badges, and War Cries*, p. 2.

blue lions, blue boars, &c., which are quite unknown to men
of science, and have never yet been seen except in Heraldry
and upon sign-boards.   A calculation will show that no less
than 203 Essex signs, or about 15 per cent., are described
as being of some particular colour, and that these coloured
signs are animals in nearly all cases—one good proof of their
heraldic origin.   Black occurs 24 times, blue 7 times, golden
6 times, green 28 times (including dragons and men only), red
39 times (including 34 RED LIONS, 3 RED COWS, 1 RED
HOUSE, and 1 RED TAPE TAVERN), and white exactly 100
times (including 50 WHITE HARTS, 2 WHITE SWANS, 2
WHITE BEARS, WHITE LIONS, WHITE HORSES, &c.).   In
London the proportion of coloured signs is much smaller.
There are 79 distinct devices, or about 4·5 per cent. of the
entire number.

Another strong proof that many of our otherwise incomprehensible signs have been derived from Heraldry, is to be
found in the frequency with which the number *Three* appears
upon sign-boards.   No less than 35 houses in Essex (having
15 distinct signs) are known as the *three* somethings, while
other numbers only occur 12 times in all.   The following is
a complete list : There are 3 TWO BREWERS, a FOUR ASHES,
2 FIVE BELLS, 3 SIX BELLS, and 4 EIGHT BELLS.   Many of
our Essex *Threes* will be noticed hereafter.   The list includes
the signs of the THREE BLACKBIRDS, the THREE COLTS, the
THREE COMPASSES, the THREE CROWNS, the THREE CUPS,
the THREE HORSESHOES, the THREE PIGEONS, the THREE
TUNS, and several others.   Nor is this peculiarity confined to
Essex signs only.   In London the number Three gives twenty-
nine distinct devices and sixty-five signs, including repetitions
of the same device.   All other numbers put together only
give twenty-two distinct devices, or fifty-five signs.   The
author of a curious and interesting letter on the signs of
Bury, which appeared in the *Bury and Norwich Post* on June
29 and July 6, 1791, noticed this prevalence of the number
Three on sign-boards in his day, and was, he says, " inclined
to account for it from a kind of predilection there is among
sign-painters to the number Three, as we see in the Three

Horse Shoes, before mentioned, also in the Three Bulls, the Three Tuns, the Three Crowns, and the Three Goats' Heads."

Now every one acquainted with Heraldry will know how very common it is to find *three* charges of some kind or other upon an escutcheon, either alone or with an "ordinary" or some other charge between them, such as *Argent, three cinquefoils gules* for D'Arcy, *Gules, three eagles displayed or* for Band, *Gules, a fess between three bulls' heads couped or* for Torrel, &c., and there can be very little doubt that this striking abundance of the number three on our sign-boards is due, largely at least, to the frequent use of that number in Heraldry. It cannot be denied, however, that three was a favourite, or lucky, number long before the first appearance of the art of Heraldry. Messrs. Larwood and Hotten cite many instances of its use, even as far back as the time of the Assyrians and ancient Egyptians. But, in spite of this, there can be no reasonable doubt that many of our "*threes*" are derived directly from Heraldry; whilst others are probably derived from it indirectly. In the latter case the name has been bestowed recently upon his house by the landlord, because he knew it to be a very common custom to call a house the "*Three* Somethings," although of the origin of that custom he probably knew absolutely nothing. Essex examples of the former class are given above. Among those of the latter are probably our signs of the THREE ASHES, the THREE ELMS, the THREE JOLLY WHEELERS, and the THREE MARINERS.

It is, of course, more than probable that some signs, which appear to be truly heraldic in their origin, are, in reality, not derived from Heraldry at all, but have been taken direct from Nature. At the same time, the evidence is overwhelming that very many of our signs have a truly heraldic origin. Messrs. Larwood and Hotten recognize this fact to a considerable extent, and devote their third chapter, comprising as much as a tenth part of their whole work, to "Heraldic and Emblematic Signs." It appears, however, that they have in most cases erred on the side of caution, and have been too reluctant to ascribe to Heraldry the origin of any sign for which another derivation could possibly be found.

3

There is, nevertheless, much truth in the opening sentences
of their fourth chapter (p. 150), treating of "Animals and
Monsters." They say :

" It is, in many cases, impossible to draw a line of demarcation between
signs borrowed from the animal kingdom and those taken from Heraldry :
we cannot now determine, for instance, whether by the WHITE HORSE is
meant simply an *equus caballus*, or the White Horse of the Saxons, and
that of the House of Hanover ; nor whether the WHITE GREYHOUND
represented originally the supporter of the arms of Henry VII., or simply
the greyhound that courses ' poor puss ' on our meadows in the hunting-
season. For this reason this chapter has been placed as a sequel to the
heraldic signs. As a rule, fantastically-coloured animals are unquestionably of heraldic origin : their number is limited to the Lion, the Boar,
the Hart, the Dog, the Cat, the Bear, and, in a few instances, the Bull.
All other animals were generally represented in what was meant for their
natural colours."

Again, the authors very truly remark (p. 110) that—

" In pondering over this class of signs, great difficulty often arises
from the absence of all proof that the animal under consideration was
set up as a badge, and not as a representation of the actual animal. As
no amount of investigation can decide this matter, we have been somewhat profuse in our list of badges, in order that the reader should be
able to form his own opinion upon that subject. Thus, for instance, with
the first sign that offers itself, THE ANGEL AND TRUMPET, it is impossible to say whether the supporters of Richard II. gave rise to it, or
whether it represents Fame."

The late Mr. Jewitt, who had an excellent knowledge of
Heraldry, in his article already referred to, clearly recognizes
the important part which that art has played in giving origin to
many of our commonest signs ; but the same cannot be said
for Mr. Pengelly's treatise on the *Signs of Devonshire*. The
connection between Heraldry and the origin of our trade-signs
is so intimate, that no one is fully competent to discuss the
latter unless well acquainted with the former ; and, although
the signs of the 1,123 inns existing in Devonshire are carefully
classified and treated of at length by Mr. Pengelly, numerous
passages make it evident from the outset that he has little
or no knowledge of the herald's art. Consequently, his
remarks lose very much of their interest. For instance, he
says :—" So far as I have been able to discover, the HARP
AND LION at Plymouth is without parallel anywhere. Its
meaning, if it have any, seems very far to seek." Had the

writer been acquainted with Heraldry, he would have known
that a lion and a harp are the principal charges in the arms
of Scotland and Wales respectively, as shown on the backs
of our florins. Again, he says :

"Three is the popular numeral, and is not, at all times, easily accounted
for. . . . There seems to be no explanation for the THREE CRANES at
Exeter, the THREE PIGEONS at Bishop's Tawton, the THREE HORSE-
SHOES, of which there are four examples, or the THREE TUNS, met with
as many as seven times, unless we suppose the number to have some
direct or indirect allusion to the doctrine of the Trinity, or to the very
popular belief that 'Three are lucky.'"

The frequent appearance of the number three on our sign-
boards has been already explained, and the origin of its use
will be made still clearer hereafter. It is certainly true that
one of Mr. Pengelly's headings is "Heraldry," but under it
he speaks of but little else than those inns which have the
"Arms" of some person or place as their sign. In this
connection he says :

"The Devonshire inn-keepers appear to be fond of heraldic signs ;
but it may be doubted whether some of the arms they have set up are
known at the Heralds' office. There are in the county as many as 253
sign-boards—*i.e.*, 22 per cent. of the entire number—bearing arms of
some kind. There is, however, a sufficient recurrence of the same
names to reduce the number to 165 distinct signs or names of coats.
The list contains the arms of a hero who had died, and a hierarchy that
had passed away—Achilles and the Druids—before the founding of the
Heraldic System ; of royal, noble, and other distinguished personages ;
of proprietors of the soil ; of countries, counties, cities, towns, and
villages ; of trades and employments ; and of objects difficult of classification."

With Mr. Pengelly's treatment of non-heraldic signs there
is, of course, no fault to be found.

M. Edouard Fournier, in his most interesting *Histoire des
Enseignes de Paris*, makes some valuable remarks on the
connection between Trade Signs and Heraldry. The following is a translation. After stating that coats of arms
came into use at the time of the Crusades, he says :

"The first Crusade dates from the year 1090. . . . Is it not allowable
to suppose that, among the Crusaders who had taken the sign of the cross
upon their coats [of arms], there were some who, prevented from starting
upon the Crusade, displayed the cross upon their houses, as a token of
their having taken a vow, sooner or later, to proceed to the Holy Land?

This would be a rational explanation of the general and widely followed custom of using the cross as the sign of a house or a shop—Red Crosses, White Crosses, Golden and Silver Crosses, &c., which form a kind of sign-board crusade. It is impossible otherwise to explain the singular and obvious analogy which exists between the devices on the shield of arms and those on the oldest sign-boards. On the sign-boards, as upon the armorial bearings, are to be seen the same devices, borrowed from every object which has a shape or a name in the creation of God or of man ; moreover, upon the sign-boards, these figures are reproduced with the various colours and 'metals' in which they appear on the coats of arms. The only difference is in the 'field' or background upon which the figures are painted. On the sign-board this is of no importance ; while it is, on the contrary, one of the distinctive features of the coat of arms. In Louvan Geliot's *Indice Armorial* (*Armorial Index*) is to be found not only a glossary of all the words used in heraldic 'blazon,' but also the names of nearly all the devices displayed upon sign-boards. . . . In a word, sign-boards and shields of arms, both alike, display figures of everything that strikes the eye or the mind in our every-day life. . . .

" The mansions built or inhabited by noble families bore, as signs, the arms of these families, sculptured or painted, over the entrance-door. These escutcheons of the nobility, without doubt, excited the envy of the merchants, who wished also to have signs, and who, therefore, placed their trade or occupation under the protection of the shield of France, or some other shield, either of a province or even of a monastery. There was nobody to object to this, and such signs quickly multiplied in every direction."

M. Fournier next gives a long list of houses which formerly displayed armorial signs in several of the " Quartiers " of Paris. " After this enumeration [he says] it will be possible to form an idea of the multitude of signs of this kind which must have existed at the same periods in the other Quarters of Paris."

Before proceeding to discuss in detail the various signs to be met with in the county of Essex, it will be well to point out two cunningly-concealed pitfalls into which the ardent antiquary is likely to fall, unless he is careful to exercise vigilance in avoiding them.

The first of these arises from the combination of two different signs into one. Larwood and Hotten speak of such signs being " quartered," but " impaled" is a much better word, if used in its old heraldic sense. Signs of this kind first began to appear about the beginning of last century, and are still common, although less so than formerly. It is noticeable that Taylor in his *Catalogue of Tavernes*, published in 1636 (see p. 28), does not name a single impaled sign, properly so-called. In some cases, such as the EAGLE AND CHILD, the STAR AND GARTER, the GEORGE AND DRAGON, &c., the connection is at once obvious; but in the great majority no meaning or connection is apparent. In such cases it will be found best not to search too deeply for a meaning, for the good reason that none exists. The mind of Addison seems to have been considerably exercised by the signs of this kind to be seen in his day in the London streets. In an amusing letter to the *Spectator*, in 1710, he professes himself desirous of obtaining office as "Superintendent of Signs," in order that he might be able to expunge those of an unnatural kind.

"My first task, therefore [he says], should be, like that of Hercules, to clear the city from monsters. In the second place, I should forbid that creatures of jarring and incongruous natures should be joined together in the same sign ; such as the BELL AND NEAT'S TONGUE, the DOG AND GRIDIRON. The FOX AND THE GOOSE may be supposed to have met ; but what have the FOX AND SEVEN STARS to do together ? And when did the LION AND DOLPHIN ever meet except upon a sign-post ? As for the CAT AND FIDDLE, there is a conceit in it ; and I, therefore, do not intend that anything that I have here said should affect it."

Further on, he makes it plain to us how some of these strange combinations arose.

"I must, however, observe to you upon this subject [says he], that it is usual for a young tradesman, at his first setting up, to add to his own sign that of the master whom he served, as the husband, after marriage, gives a place to his mistress's arms in his own coat. This I take to have given rise to many of those absurdities which are committed over our heads ; and, as I am informed, first occasioned the THREE NUNS AND A HARE, which we see so frequently joined together."

According to Messrs. Larwood and Hotten (p. 21) impaled signs, too, were often set up " on removing from one shop to another, when it was customary to add the sign of the old shop to that of the new." Numerous examples may be cited of impaled signs which occur at the present time in Essex. Such are the BULL AND HORSESHOE (p. 65) at North Weald, the LION AND BOAR (p. 63) at Earl's Colne, the LION AND KEY (p. 63) at Leyton, the BULL AND CROWN (p. 65) at Chingford, the STAR AND. FLEECE (p. 79) at

Kelvedon, the SUN AND WHALEBONE (p. 83) at Latton, the
examples of the COCK AND BELL (p. 99) at Writtle, Romford,
and High Easter, the RAINBOW AND DOVE (p. 101) at North
Weald, the CROWN AND BLACKSMITH (p. 131) at Tendring,
the examples of the PLOW AND SAIL (p. 146) at Tollesbury,
East Hanningfield, Paglesham, and Maldon, the SUN AND
ANCHOR (p. 147) at Steeple, the BELL AND ANCHOR (p. 159)
at Canning Town, the COACH AND BELL (p. 159) at Romford,
the OLD WINDMILL AND BELLS (p. 159) also at Romford, the
CROWN AND CROOKED BILLET (p. 162) at Woodford Bridge,
and many others. These will all be found noticed in their
proper places. Many other apparently impaled signs might
be noticed. Such are the COACH AND HORSES (p. 57), the
LION AND LAMB (p. 63), the EAGLE AND CHILD (p. 92), the
DOG AND PARTRIDGE (p. 75), the ROSE AND CROWN (p. 116),
the GEORGE AND DRAGON (p. 128), &c., &c. ; but these do not
properly belong to this class, there being some obvious or
possible connection between the two objects named in each
case. Among signs of this kind—apparently, though not
strictly speaking, impaled—belong all, or most, combinations
of any object with either a Hand or a Hoop. Such are the
HAND AND GLOVE (p. 142), the HAND AND BALL (p. 142), the
CROSS AND HAND (p. 142), and the HAND AND STAR (p. 28); also
the COCK AND HOOP, the HOOP AND HORSESHOE, the HOOP AND
GRAPES, which do not occur in Essex. Combinations with a
Hand generally arose from the fact that it was once common
to represent on the sign-board a hand holding or supporting
some other object. In many cases, no doubt, such combinations originally represented some family crest, in which (as
is commonly the case) a hand supported a cross, a glove, a
spear, or some other object as the case might be. Combinations into which a Hoop enters may be explained by
mentioning the fact that formerly the sign was not always
painted on a board, but often carved in wood or metal and
suspended before the house within a hoop.

The second cause of difficulty arises from the fact that
some signs have become altered and corrupted in the course
of time. Many curious examples of signs of this class are

given by the authors so often quoted. Most of them seem to have arisen in this way :—A sign was put up which com-memorated some incident or personage, often perhaps of only local celebrity. In the course of time the occurrence commemorated or the individual represented by the sign became forgotten (or, at any rate, disconnected from the sign) ; and, under the influence of vulgar pronunciation (or, possibly, upon the advent of a fresh landlord, who knew nothing as to the significance of the old name), the sign was changed, and given some fresh meaning, which the words seemed to imply or nearly resemble. Such signs as these may be styled "corruptions." As an example, it may be mentioned that at Hever, in Kent, near which place the Bullen or Boleyn family had large possessions, there was, for many years after the death of the unfortunate Ann, an ale-house with the sign of the BULLEN BUTCHERED; but, on the place falling into fresh hands, the sign was vulgarized into the BULL AND BUTCHER (!), and so remained until a recent date. In exactly the same way, a farm standing on or near the site of one of the old lodges at one of the entrances to the Park of New Hall, Boreham—another ancient estate of the Boleyn or Bullen family—is now known as "Bull's Lodge Farm," it having formerly been "Bullen's Lodge Farm." Thus, too, the GEORGE CANNING has become changed into the GEORGE AND CANNON, the ISLAND QUEEN into the ICELAND QUEEN, the FOUR ALLS into the FOUR AWLS (and used as a shoemaker's sign), and the ELEPHANT AND CASTLE into the PIG AND TINDERBOX. It is by no means improbable that, if sufficiently minute inquiry were to be made, it would be found that some of our 22 Essex SHIPS, many of which are situated far from the sea, and in purely agricultural districts, are intended for *Sheep*, that word being, in Essex, invariably pronounced "ship," both in the singular and plural. The Stock SHIP, for instance, occupies some of the highest ground in the county, and is a well-known land-mark for many miles around. It could hardly have reached its present position without undergoing some such strange adventures as Noah's Ark is said to have experienced. The

authors of the *History of Sign-boards* state that the two words
"ship" and "sheep" were once commonly pronounced almost
promiscuously, as now in Essex. At Berkhampstead, in Hertfordshire, moreover, there is a house which formerly had a
pictorial representation of a ship in full sail as its sign. Of
late, however, the sign-board has merely borne the word
"ship;" and, quite recently, on the advent of a new landlord who had been a cattle-dealer, the sign was changed
into the SHEEP. On the other hand, there is, at Chipping

Norton, in Oxfordshire, a house styled
the SHEEP AND ANCHOR, which, doubtless, should be, and originally was,
the SHIP AND ANCHOR. The old sign
of the FALCON AND FETTERLOCK, representing the badge of John of Ghent, is
now often corrupted into the HAWK AND
BUCKLE, or even into the HAWK AND

FALCON AND FETTERLOCK. BUCK. In speaking of Essex examples
of corrupted signs, it may be mentioned that the GOAT AND
BOOTS (p. 81) appears at Colchester for the GOAT IN BOOTS,
and that the DE BEAUVOIR'S ARMS (p. 43) at Downham is
locally known as "the BEAVERS." In the *Post Office Directory*, too, the HORSE AND WELL (p. 57) at Woodford
appears as the HORSE AND WHEEL, the ROMAN URN (p. 44)
at Colchester as the ROMAN ARMS, and the SUNDERLAND ARMS
(p. 31) at Wakes Colne as the SUTHERLAND ARMS. Some
of these are not corruptions which have actually taken place
on the sign-board; but they well show the tendency towards
such corruption. There can be but little doubt, too, that the
sign of the HARROW (p. 171) represents the *Portcullis crowned*
which Henry VII. and other sovereigns used as a badge.
When the knowledge of heraldry declined the common
people called the sign by the name of the Harrow, not
knowing of anything else which resembled the device displayed. It thus became an agricultural sign, and was sometimes combined with another sign of the same kind, namely,
the PLOUGH, as at Leytonstone (p. 170). In other counties,
according to Larwood and Hotten, the sign is still com-

monly known as the PORTCULLIS, but we have no example in Essex. Some forty years ago it was recorded in the *Worcester Journal* that the landlord of the WHITE HART Inn at Dudley decided that his sign, which had until then been merely written, should be made pictorial; but instead of having depicted the ordinary White Hart with golden chain and collar, he (whether through ignorance or intent) had painted in white, on a black ground, a large Elephant's *Heart!* Of this absurd corruption we have now an example in Essex, as mentioned hereafter (p. 53).

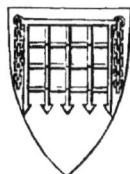

PORTCULLIS.

It was also once a very common thing for the sign to form a " rebus," or pun, upon the name of the owner. Thus Two COCKS represented Cox; THREE CONIES, Conny; THREE FISHES, Fish, &c., &c. The token issued in 1665 by "Beniamin Samson in Coggeshall" bears what Boyne describes as "the figure of Sampson, standing, with a robe over his shoulder and loins, holding a jawbone in one hand." Many combinations, otherwise inexplicable, doubtless arose from this source, such as a HAND AND COCK, signifying Hancock, and a BABE AND TUN, signifying Babington. It is not easy to detect any instance in which a rebus or punning device now appears on an Essex sign-board; but several cases may be pointed out on the trade-tokens issued by Essex tradesmen in the seventeenth century. Thus, a LAMB appears on the token of Thomas Lambe of Colchester in 1654 (p. 80), a FINCH on that of John Finch of Halstead, and a TREE on that of W. Spiltimber of Hatfield Broad Oak. It is worth mention, too, that Mr. A. Stagg, an English hatter, in the Rue Auber, Paris, displays two gilded stags' heads on the facia above his shop.

Thus we see that, in searching for the origin of any sign of obscure derivation, we may have to trace it back through several different forms.

Coming now to the more particular examination of the signs connected with Essex, we find that the signs of the 1,355 inns existing in the county furnish an ample fund of interest to any one who systematically studies their origin and significance. For convenience in treatment an attempt has been made to arrange these signs under various headings, and under one or other of these headings every distinct inn-sign now appearing in the county will be found treated of, together with a large number of other signs which once existed in Essex, but have now disappeared. The list of Essex inns given in the *Post Office Directory* for the county has been found very useful, although, unfortunately, the signs of the numerous "beer-shops" (when they have any) are not given. This deficiency has, however, to some extent, been supplied through the kindness of the magistrates' clerks in the county, who have forwarded lists of such beer-houses as have signs or names in their respective divisions. The information thus obtained has been incorporated with the remainder; but in speaking of a certain sign appearing so many times in the county the number of fully-licensed houses alone is in all. cases referred to. In various parts of the county, but especially in the south-western portion round Epping and Ongar (as also in London), these houses are known among the labouring people by the strange name of "Tom and Jerrys," no explanation of the origin of which seems to be obtainable. Beer-houses are compelled by Act of Parliament (1 Will. IV., c. 64, s. 6, & 4 & 5 Will. IV., c. 85, s. 18) to display over their doors a descriptive board, to be "publicly visible and legible," under penalty of £10, but it does not appear that either they or fully-licensed houses are compelled to display signs.

There does not appear to have been any complete list of the inns of the county published more than forty years ago, but even the lists extending back that far may advantageously be compared with that of the present time. Although very many of our signs still remain the same now as they were then, numerous changes are noticeable. These are, however, generally in the direction that might be expected. Old heraldic devices are slowly disappearing and giving place to modern vulgarisms. For instance, so lately as the year 1868 RAILWAY INNS and RAILWAY TAVERNS combined only numbered twenty, while at the present time we have no less than thirty-one. It is quite clear that in the early part of this century, before railways came into existence, these signs must have been altogether unknown. Their places were then filled by such signs as the COACH AND HORSES or the HORN AND HORSESHOES, and other signs now going out of fashion.

A great deal of very useful and interesting information as to the signs in use in Essex two centuries ago is also to be obtained from an examination of the list of seventeenth-century tokens given by Mr. Boyne.[1] These tokens were issued very numerously by tradesmen during the Common-wealth and the reign of Charles I., when the national coinage was in an extremely debased condition. In the "field," or centre, of the coin there was generally a device, which usually represented the sign under which the issuer traded. Many of the objects thus represented have, of course, disappeared from the sign-boards of the present day, though very many others are still familiar public-house signs. Mr. Boyne is, however, of the opinion that not more than one-fifth of the tokens now extant were issued by tavern-keepers, the rest having been circulated by ordinary tradesmen. Reference has already been made to the fact that many of the common heraldic signs had their origin in the use formerly made of the arms of the various Trade Guilds or companies as signs; and a hasty examination of the list of Essex tokens given by Boyne shows that between 80 and 90, or 37 per cent., bear arms or emblems belonging to one or other of these ancient companies. Thus, the Grocers appear about 25 times, the Bakers about 13 times, the Tallow-chandlers 10 times, the Woolmen 8 times, the Clothworkers 4 times, the Blacksmiths and the Drapers each 3 times, the Mercers, the Apothecaries, and the Barber Surgeons each twice, and the Brewers, the Fishmongers, the Butchers, the Fruiterers, and the Cutlers each once. Each of these signs will be hereafter treated of in its proper place.

---

[1] *Tokens Issued in the Seventeenth Century*, &c. By William Boyne, F.S.A. London, 1858.

A very interesting list of the inns in Essex (107 in all) in 1636 is given in John Taylor's—the "Water Poet's"— *Catalogue of Tavernes in Tenne Shires about London*, published in that year.   Unfortunately, however, in only thirteen cases does he give the sign.   In all other cases he merely gives the name of the holder.   Frequent allusion will hereafter be made to this list of inns.

In the first edition of *Pigot's Commercial Directory*, published in 1823, is a list of the inns in the principal Essex towns at that ·day, which has proved very useful.   An asterisk placed before the sign of any particular existing inn, or the name of the place at which it is situated, indicates that the inn in question is mentioned in the above *Directory*, and that it is therefore at least 64 years old.

It is much to be regretted that, although the inns are, as a rule, among the oldest and most interesting houses in any small town or country village, our Essex historians have, almost without exception, been too fully occupied in tracing the descent of manors and estates, even to notice them.

The list given in the *London Directory* for 1885 enumerates no less than 1,742 distinct signs or devices, as appearing in the metropolis alone.   Some of these are, of course, repeated as many as fifty times.

HAND AND STAR.
(*Date* 1550, *after Larwood and Hotten.*)

CHAPTER II.

HERALDIC SIGNS.

. . . "a coat of arms, . . . and wild beasts on their hind legs, showing it, as if it
was a copy they had done, with mouths from ear to ear,—good gracious !"
DICKENS : *Little Dorrit*, book ii., chap. ix.

S the quaint art of Heraldry has given to us
many, if not a majority, of our most interesting signs, it is only reasonable that
signs of this class should be treated first.
In all respects the most purely heraldic
sign we have in Essex is the FLEUR-DE-LYS,
which occurs at Widdington. As a sign, this was formerly
much more common than at present. Eight of the Essex
tokens are described as having borne it. Two of these were
issued in Colchester, two in Billericay, and one each in
Chelmsford, Coggeshall, Stock, and Witham, the issuer at
the latter place being John Jackson, clothier, in 1669. There
was formerly a house of this name at Waltham Abbey. In
the parish register the burial of a landlord, on May 8, 1684,
is recorded as follows :—" Edward Clarke, att ye flower de
luis." Mr. H. W. King, too, finds mention in ancient deeds
of a " Flower de Luce " at Maldon in 1658, and again in
1690, but whether an inn, shop, or dwelling-house, there is, as
usual, no evidence to show. As it is sometimes varied into
the THREE FLEURS DE LYS, the most reasonable conclusion
is that it is taken from the arms of France, as formerly quartered with those of England, but a fleur-de-lys was also used
as a badge by Edward III. In former times, too, it was an
emblem of the Virgin Mary. In London at the present day
the sign occurs once only, namely, in Fleur-de-Lys Street, E.

Below are depicted four of the many forms taken by this
device on early shields of arms.

FLEUR DE LYS (*four early forms*).

No less than 116 of our present public-houses (or 8·5 per
cent.) are named after the arms of some family, place, city,
country, or trade. Those obviously named after some place
within the county will be first noticed. To commence with,
however, we will mention the ROYAL ARMS
at Silvertown.[1] The same device appears
on a token inscribed "Theophilus Harvey,
in Manitree, 1669." Next we have the ESSEX
ARMS.[2] There are now four examples, though
forty years ago there were five. At Springfield, too, there is a beer-house of this name.

ESSEX ARMS.

Then we have a *COLCHESTER ARMS,[3] which is, of course,
situated at Colchester. It is at least forty
years old. The COLCHESTER ARMS also
appear on the halfpenny token of Alexander
Satterthwaite, of Colchester, dated 1668.
The BOROUGH ARMS at Maldon are, of
course, the arms of that town.[4] The ABBEY
ARMS at Plaistow doubtless represent the
arms of the neighbouring Abbey of Barking.[5] Sixty years

COLCHESTER ARMS.

[1] Quarterly: first and fourth, gules; three lions passant guardant in
pale, or, for England, &c.

[2] These are commonly blazoned as follows, but they belong equally to
Middlesex, and in reality no county possesses arms :—Gules, three seaxes
proper, hilts and pomels or, points to sinister.

[3] Gules; two staves raguly and couped, one in pale surmounted by
another in fess, both argent, between two ducal coronets in chief or, and
the bottom of the staff enfiled with another ducal of the last.

[4] Azure; three lions passant, regardant, in pale or.

[5] Azure; three roses, two and one, in base, or; in chief as many lilies,
argent, stalked and leaved vert; all within a bordure gules charged with
eight plates.

ago there was a HARWICH ARMS[1] at *Harwich. Then
we have the HUTTON ARMS at Hutton, the CHADWELL
ARMS at Chadwell Heath, the BERECHURCH ARMS at Lexden, the ROMFORD ARMS (beer-house) at Romford, the
COLNE VALLEY ARMS at Birdbrook, and the ROYAL ESSEX
ARMS at Braintree, all of which coats the heralds would
probably be unable to find entered at Heralds' College. The
last-named is an especially strange device. It is probably an
impaled sign, due to a combination of the ROYAL ARMS and
the ESSEX ARMS.

Many other of our "arms" are named after places outside
the county. Probably in many cases a new landlord has
named his house after the place he came from. Such are the
CAMBRIDGE ARMS, the CUCKFIELD ARMS, the DARTMOUTH
ARMS, the DENMARK ARMS, the DORSET ARMS, 2 DURHAM
ARMS, the FALMOUTH ARMS, the IPSWICH ARMS, the LIVER-
POOL ARMS, the NORTHUMBERLAND ARMS, the ODESSA ARMS,
the LILLIPUT ARMS (in the Lilliput Road, Stratford), the
TOWER HAMLETS ARMS (at Forest Gate), and the KENT
ARMS at North Woolwich, a parish belonging to Kent,
though situated on the north side of the river. Twenty years
ago there was also a SUSSEX ARMS in existence. The CITY
ARMS at Canning Town presumably represent the arms of
the City of London.[2] The dagger in the City arms commemorates the slaying of Wat Tyler by Sir William Wal-
worth, in 1381. The weapon used is still in the possession
of the Fishmongers' Company. The SUTHERLAND ARMS at
Wakes Colne seems from the printed list to have been
corrupted from the SUNDERLAND ARMS within the last
twenty years. An example of both forms occurs in London
at the present time. It is most probable that some of these
signs have not taken their names direct from the counties or
towns mentioned, but from the titles of noblemen who have
become prominent for political or other reasons. This has

---

[1] Gules; a portcullis with chains pendant, or, nailed and pointed
azure.
[2] Argent; a cross of St. George; cantoned in the first quarter, a
dagger erect, gules.

been almost certainly the case with the CAMBRIDGE ARMS, the DURHAM ARMS, and the LIVERPOOL ARMS.

The following signs are, with equal clearness, derived from trades or employments pursued within the county. Many of them are, doubtless, derived directly from the arms of the London Trade Companies. Of the BLACKSMITHS' ARMS [1] we have examples situated respectively at Little Clacton and at North Weald. The Blacksmiths' Arms also appear on the halfpenny tokens of "Will Todd, Blacksmith of Epping," 1668, and of William Thompson of South Benfleet (no date). The BLACKSMITHS' ARMS, at Little Clacton, appears to have existed since 1786 at least, as it is referred to in an advertisement in the *Chelmsford Chronicle* for March 17th in that year. Not improbably the HAMMER AND PINCERS crossed, which appeared on the halfpenny of Will Willis of Romford, in 1667, constituted a blacksmith's sign.

The BREWERS' ARMS [2] occur as a sign at Woodham Ferris and *Colchester. The THREE TUNS, of which we have examples at Newport, *Dunmow, and Waltham Abbey, all of them being at least forty years old, are certainly derived from the arms either of the Brewers' Company or the Vintners' Company.[3] THREE TUNS are depicted on the token issued by William Harman, of Chelmsford, in 1657.

BREWERS' ARMS.

The THREE TUNS which formerly existed at *Chelmsford was long a well-known inn. The Rev. R. E. Bartlett finds it mentioned in the parish registers in 1619, when "a chrisome son of Robt. Ogden of Chelmsford, Vintner, at the 3 Tunnes, and of Susan his wife, was buried the xxx day of December, being Thurs-

[1] Sable ; a chevron or, between three hammers argent, handled of the second, ducally crowned of the last.
[2] Gules ; on a chevron argent between three pair of barley garbs in saltire or, three tuns sable, hooped of the third.
[3] Sable ; a chevron between three tuns argent.

day." Taylor also mentions it in his *Catalogue of Tavernes,* published in 1636. Sixty years ago there was a house of this name at *Braintree, and in 1789 that at Waltham Abbey was spelled THREE TONS. The Bakers' Arms[1] occur on the tokens some thirteen times, either as the BAKERS' ARMS, a HAND AND SCALES, a PAIR OF SCALES, or a PAIR OF SCALES AND A WHEATSHEAF. The BAKERS' ARMS now only appears as an inn-sign at Leyton, but there are beer-houses of this name at Buttsbury and Waltham Abbey. Our common modern sign of the WHEATSHEAF is also probably derived from the arms of this Company. There are seven examples in the county, situated respectively at Wrabness, *Chelmsford, Tolleshunt D'Arcy, Braintree, Stow Maries, High Ongar, and Ardleigh. There are also beer-houses of this name at Loughton, Theydon Bois, Waltham Abbey, Hatfield Peverell, Kelvedon, Rettendon, Writtle, Hornchurch, &c. A house at Castle Hedingham, known as the WHEATSHEAF, though now a beer-shop merely, appears once to have been a very good private residence. The WHEATSHEAF at *Chelmsford seems to have been in existence since 1786 at least, as it is mentioned in the *Chelmsford Chronicle* on January 13th in that year. Likewise the still-extant sign of the MAID'S HEAD (to be noticed hereafter) is probably derived from the arms of the Mercers' Company,[2] which appear on the undated farthings of "Thomas Bvrges, Est Street, Covlchester," and "Clement Pask of Castell Heninhame." The MASONS' ARMS[3] occur at *Moulsham. The GARDENERS' ARMS[4] appear at Wakes Colne and Loughton (beer-house). The WHEELERS' ARMS[5] (? *Wheelwrights' Arms*) appear at

---

[1] Gules ; a balance between three garbs or ; on a chief, a hand supporting the balance, &c.

[2] Gules ; a demi-virgin couped below the shoulders, issuing from clouds all proper, vested or, crowned with an eastern crown of the last, her hair dishevelled and wreathed around the temples with roses of the second, all within an orle of clouds proper.

[3] Azure ; on a chevron between three towers argent, a pair of compasses open sable.

[4] A landscape, the base variegated with flowers, a man proper, vested round the loins with linen argent, digging with a spade, all of the first.

[5] Gules ; a chevron between three wheels, or, on a chief argent, an axe lying fessways proper.

4

Good Easter.   The BRICKLAYERS' ARMS [1] occur three
times, namely, at Colchester, Stondon, and Bocking (beer-
shop).   The ROYAL HOTEL at Purfleet is famed for its
whitebait.   Until recently it was known as the BRICK-
LAYERS' ARMS, evidently, as Mr. Palin thinks,[2] because
the Bricklayers' Company formerly worked the huge chalk
quarries close at hand.   The BUTCHERS' ARMS [3] occur at
Wimbish, Felstead, Stambourne, and Woodham Ferris (beer-
shop).   Probably the BULL'S HEAD, the BOAR'S HEAD, and
the FLY AND BULLOCK, to be noticed hereafter, are all

BUTCHERS' ARMS.

connected with the arms of this Company, which appear
on the halfpenny of " John Harvey of Rochfoord " in 1668.
The CARPENTERS' ARMS [4] occur eight times in the county,

[1] Azure ; a chevron or ; in chief a fleur-de-lys argent between two brick
axes paleways of the second ; in base a bundle of laths of the last.
[2] *More about Stifford*, p. 95.
[3] Azure; two slaughter axes indorsed in saltire argent, handled or,
between three bulls' heads couped of the second, two in fess, one in base ;
on a chief argent, a boar's head couped, gules, between two block-brushes
vert.
[4] Argent; a chevron engrailed between three pairs of compasses,
extended, sable.

and also often serve as a beer-house sign. One near Chelmsford is kept by a carpenter, as is, doubtless, often the case.
There can be no doubt that the COMPASSES, which occurs
six times, and the THREE COMPASSES, which appears twice,
are derived from the arms of this Company. A house near
Waltham Abbey, now known by the latter form of the
sign, seems in 1789 to have been called the COMPASSES
merely. The AXE AND COMPASSES at Arkesden is probably
a modern, but certainly an appropriate, combination ; or the
axe may be intended for one of the adzes in the arms of the
Coopers' Company, for the COOPERS' ARMS[1] themselves
appear at Chadwell Heath, Aldham, Chelmsford, and Romford, the last two being beer-houses. Although the arms of the
Cutlers' Company[2] are not now to be seen on our sign-boards,
there can be little doubt that the TWO SWORDS CROSSED,
which appeared on the undated farthing of "Nathaniell Smith
in Thacksteed," were derived from the arms of that Company,
Thaxted having formerly been a seat of the cutlery trade, as
the name "Cutlers' Green," in the immediate vicinity, indicates. The WATERMAN'S ARMS[3] was formerly a sign at
Leigh, but whether of an inn or private house does not appear. Mr. H. W. King is able, by means of evidence obtained
from old deeds, to give a complete account of the house
which displayed this sign (and which was built about the
time of Charles I.) from 1650 ; but there are earlier notices
of it. Portions of it, built of oak, are still standing, but
much altered. When it first became an inn does not appear.
It is first mentioned as having been such in 1746, when it is
described as "two tenements now and lately called the
Waterman's Arms." Probably, therefore, it had even then
ceased to be an inn, and had been divided into two dwelling-

---

[1] Gyronny of eight, gules and sable ; on a chevron between three annu-
lets or, a grose between two adzes azure ; on a chief vert, three lilies
slipped, stalked and leaved argent.
[2] Gules ; three pairs of swords in saltire argent, hilts and pomels or,
two pair in chief and one in base.
[3] Barry-wavy of six, argent and azure ; on the middle bar a boat, or ;
on a chief of the second two bars in saltire, of the third, between two
cushions of the first, tasselled or.

houses. Under the floor of one of the rooms, some years
since, were found several small coins of Charles II., and a
leaden tavern token, undated, but probably of the seventeenth
century. On it was a hand or arm, pouring from a tankard into
a cup or glass. Forty years ago there was a POULTERERS'
ARMS [1] at Chelmsford. Larwood and Hotten do not notice
this sign.

Similarly, several other Companies, whose arms are not
now to be found named upon our Essex sign-boards, appear
to have given us signs which we still have. For instance,
the sign of the TROWEL AND HAMMER at Marks Tey (which

THE CUPS HOTEL, COLCHESTER.

is not mentioned by Larwood and Hotten) is in all probability derived from the arms of the Plasterers' Company,[2]
while the sign of THREE CUPS has, doubtless, been derived from the arms of the Salters' Company.[3] Of this sign
we have examples at Great Oakley, Maldon, Springfield, and
*Colchester. The THREE CUPS at Colchester (commonly

---

[1] Argent; on a chevron between three storks gules, as many swans
proper.

[2] Azure; on a chevron engrailed or, between two plasterers' hammers
and a trowel argent in chief and a flat brush in base, a rose, &c.

[3] Per chevron, azure and gules; three covered sprinkling-salts argent.

called the CUPS), though not one of the oldest licensed houses in that ancient borough, was long a well-known coaching inn, and for upwards of half a century has been the leading hotel in the town. There is reason to believe that a small tavern known as the Queen's Head stood upon the site in the days of Elizabeth; but a more commodious building was erected, as an inscription on the front stated, in 1792. That, however, had become too antiquated for its requirements, and was demolished in 1885. Upon its site has now been erected an extremely handsome building of brick and stone. Carved on one of the projecting windows are " three cups," with pedestals, but they do not correctly represent the " covered sprinkling-salts " of the Salters' Arms. These, however, are correctly represented, being carved in wood, and supported upon a sign-post, before the THREE CUPS at *Springfield, a house at least a century old, as it is mentioned in the *Chelmsford Chronicle* on March 30, 1787.

In a curious poem, describing a journey from London to Aldborough and back, published in 1804,[1] the THREE CUPS at *Harwich—now known as the CUPS—is thus alluded to :

> " But now we're at Harwich, and thankful am I,
> Our Inn's the Three Cups, and our dinner draws nigh,
> But first for a walk to survey this old Borough,
> To peep at the church, and the churchyard go thorough."

Again, the ADAM AND EVE, which occurs at West Ham, as noticed hereafter, is a very old device as a sign. This example is forty years old at least. Messrs. Larwood and Hotten state (p. 257) that " our first parents were constant *dramatis personæ* in the mediæval mysteries and pageants ; " but both they and Mr. Jewitt overlook the fact that the sign may with equal probability have been derived from the arms of the Fruiterers' Company,[2] which appear on the halfpenny of Jasper Eve of Springfield in 1669. In this case, however,

---

[1] Journal of a very young Lady's Tour from Canonbury to Aldborough, through Chelmsford, Sudbury, and Ipswich, and back through Harwich, Colchester, &c., September 13-21, 1804. Only 24 copies printed. 16 pp., 8vo.

[2] Azure ; on a mount in base vert, the tree of paradise environed with the serpent between Adam and Eve, all proper.

the device probably was intended as a rebus upon the name. The sign of the THREE PIGEONS is not improbably derived from the arms of the Tallow-chandlers' Company,[1] since there is no other obvious source from which it can have come. Although Larwood and Hotten seem to regard it as being now a rare sign, there are two cases of it in Essex—one at Stratford, and the other at Halstead. As already stated, the occupation of the tallow-chandler is represented ten times on the Essex tokens of the seventeenth century, either by the arms of the Company, by a man making candles, or by a stick of candles. The latter device appears on the undated farthing of William Newman of Halstead, and may have some connection with the THREE PIGEONS which now exists there, and has certainly done so for at least forty years back. The DOVE AND OLIVE-BRANCH, which is shown on the undated farthing of " George Evanes in Ingatestone," is also probably a device taken from the arms of this Company. Other arms and emblems belonging to the great trade companies, and appearing commonly on the tokens of the seventeenth century, have now quite disappeared—at least so far as Essex is concerned. For instance, the BARBER-SURGEONS' ARMS[2] are to be seen on the halfpence of " Thomas Bvll of Mamvdine, 1669," and of " Henry Carter, Chirvrgeon, in Manitree, 1669." The GROCERS' ARMS[3] occur, as already stated, no less than about twenty-five times, either as the Grocers' Arms, a sugar-loaf, three sugar-loaves, one or more cloves, or a sugar-loaf and cloves combined. The GROCERS' ARMS and an ESCALOP occur respectively on the two sides of the undated token of "George Nicholson in Tolshon Dacey in S.X." The sign of the THREE SUGAR-LOAVES still occurs at Sible Hedingham, and has been in existence there for a century at least, as the house is mentioned in an advertisement in the *Chelmsford*

[1] Per fess, azure and argent ; a pale counter-changed ; three doves of the last, each holding in the beak an olive-branch or.

[2] Quarterly ; first and fourth sable ; a chevron between three fleams argent ; second and third per pale, argent and vert, &c.

[3] Argent ; a chevron gules between nine cloves sable, three, three and three.

Chronicle on March 9, 1787. It can hardly be called an heraldic sign, as the three sugar-loaves seem only to have been set up by grocers as an emblem of their business. At the present time the house has no sign-board, but the three sugar-loaves are suspended over the door as here shown. There is also a beer-house of the same name in Felstead parish.

The WOOLPACK, which occurs eight times on the Essex tokens of the seventeenth century, and six times in the

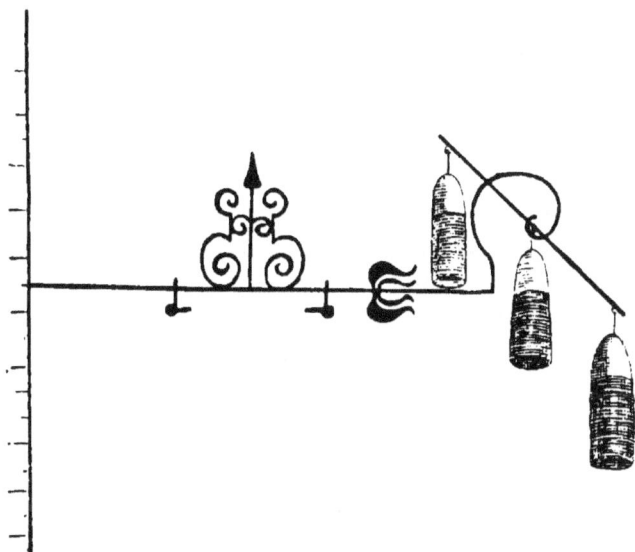

THREE SUGAR-LOAVES AT SIBLE HEDINGHAM.

county at present, will be noticed hereafter. It is, doubtless, derived from the arms of the Woolmen's Company.[1] The APOTHECARIES' ARMS[2] appear on the tokens of "Isaac Colman, grocr, in Colchester, 1667," and of Thomas Bradshawe of Harwich, in the same year. The DRAPERS' ARMS[3]

[1] Gules ; a woolpack argent.
[2] Azure ; Apollo proper, a bow in left hand and an arrow in the right or, supplanting a serpent argent.
[3] Azure ; three clouds proper, radiated in base, or each surmounted with a triple crown or.

occur three times on the Essex tokens. The sign of the THREE CROWNS, which occurs four times in the county, as hereafter

DRAPERS' ARMS.

mentioned, is very probably derived either from the arms of the Drapers' Company, or from those of the Skinners' Company.[1] The signs of the HORSESHOE and the THREE HORSESHOES (the former of which occurs three times in the county and the latter ten times) probably both owe their origin partly to the fact that horseshoes appear on the arms of the Farriers' Company,[2] and partly to the old custom of fastening a horseshoe upon the stable-door or elsewhere in the belief that it would scare away witches. The THREE HORSESHOES now existing at Billericay seems to be at least one hundred years old, [as it is referred to in the *Chelmsford Chronicle* on March 10, 1786. As a beer-house sign the HORSESHOE occurs at Great Parndon, and the THREE HORSESHOES at Braintree, Waltham Abbey, High Ongar, and elsewhere. It appears from the parish registers of Grays that there was a HORSESHOES there in 1724, and there was a THREE HORSESHOES at Great Parndon in 1789. The CLOTHWORKERS' ARMS [3] appear twice on the Colchester tokens, once on the farthing of " William Cant, in Hedingham Sibley, 1667," and once elsewhere. The SHUTTLE on the tokens of " Moses Love, slaymaker, of Coggshall," and " Nathaniell Cattlin of Safron Walden, 1668," the WOMAN SPINNING on that of " John Little in Movlshem, 1666," and the pair of SHEARS on that of " James Bonvm in Stisted, 1670," are all probably connected with the woollen trade which formerly flourished in Essex. In 1662 there was a

[1] Ermine ; on a chief gules, three princes' crowns composed of crosses pattée and fleurs-de-lys or.

[2] Argent ; three horseshoes sable, pierced of the field.

[3] Sable ; a chevron ermine between two habicks in chief argent and a teazle in base, slipped, or.

house known as the SHEARS in Chelmsford. It is mentioned in the *Account of the Murder of Thomas Kidderminster* as being in " Colchester-lane," which was probably what is now known as Springfield Lane. Littlebury was once another seat of the woollen trade. Until comparatively recently the 3rd of February used to be celebrated there, as related in a poem still occasionally to be met with, that being the day dedicated to Bishop Blaize, patron of workers in wool. Two huge pairs of shears, one of which is here represented, may still be seen carved on the old oaken north door of the church.

SHEARS.
(*From Littlebury Church Door.*)

In addition to the foregoing signs connected with trades and occupations, we have the following, though none of the employments named ever bore coats of arms. Most of them are modern vulgarisms, and need no further attention. There are CRICKETERS' ARMS at Manningtree, Danbury, and Rickling; MALTSTERS' ARMS at Willingale Doe, Lambourne (beer-house), and Colchester; FREEMASONS' ARMS at Brightlingsea and Braintree (beer-house); a DROVERS' ARMS at Rayleigh; an ENGINEERS' ARMS at Stratford; THATCHERS' ARMS at Mount Bures and Rettendon (beer-shop), Tolleshunt D'Arcy, and Great Warley; a VOLUNTEERS' ARMS at Maldon; a YACHTSMAN'S ARMS at Brightlingsea; a SLATERS' ARMS at Chadwell Heath; a MOULDERS' ARMS (beer-shop) at Great Wakering; a WOODCUTTERS' ARMS (beer-shop) at Eastwood; a FOUNDRY ARMS (beer-shop) at Hornchurch (of course named after Messrs. Wedlake's foundry there); LABOURERS' ARMS at Great Baddow and Woodham Ferris (beer-shops); and an ODD FELLOWS' ARMS at Springfield (beer-house). Mr. H. W. King finds mention in ancient deeds of a house at Leigh, in 1682, with the sign of the HAMBRO' MERCHANTS' ARMS, but whether an inn, shop, or private residence does not appear, nor is there any subsequent mention of it. The owner, George King, is described as a mercer on some of his tokens, still extant, and also on his tombstone, now destroyed. Most probably, therefore, it was a shop-sign. It stood on the site of the present KING'S HEAD. At High Ongar a beer-shop displays the sign of the FORESTERS' ARMS. Sixty years ago there was a NELSON'S ARMS at *Colchester. At the same time, the WEAVERS' ARMS[1] formed a very suitable sign at *Colchester, and there were a *JOINERS' ARMS, a *TAILORS' ARMS, and a *SAWYERS' ARMS at the same place. Of the latter, there is still an example (beer-house) at Magdalen Laver. In times past, probably, many other trades have had their "Arms," though only sign-board ones.

Many other "arms" are borrowed from the names of illustrious persons, though there is some uncertainty about several in the subjoined list. The following will be at once seen to be named after well-known Essex landowners : such are, the DUCANE ARMS at Braxted, the LENNARD ARMS at Aveley, the NEVILLE ARMS at Audley End, the RAYLEIGH ARMS at Terling, the TOWER ARMS at South Weald, the WAKE ARMS at Waltham Abbey (which is over forty years old), the WILKES ARMS at Wenden Lofts, and the WESTERN ARMS at Rivenhall, which figured as the LORD WESTERN ARMS forty years ago, when there was also a PETRE'S ARMS at Ingatestone. Other arms of this class, but not necessarily connected with the county, are the CAMDEN ARMS at Forest Gate, the COWLEY ARMS at Leytonstone, the HEADLEY ARMS at Great Warley, the HENLEY ARMS at North Wool-wich, the LAURIE ARMS at Romford, the MANBY ARMS and the WADDINGTON ARMS at Stratford, the MILTON ARMS at Southend, the SPENCERS' ARMS at Hornchurch, and the DE BEAUVOIRS' ARMS at Downham, together with the PETO ARMS, the SIDNEY ARMS, the SUTTON ARMS, and two NAPIER'S ARMS. Sixty years ago there was a *THEOBALD'S

---

[1] Azure ; on a chevron argent between three leopards' heads, each having in the mouth a shuttle or, as many roses gules, seeded of the third, barbed vert.

ARMS at Grays. The DE BEAUVOIRS' ARMS is at least forty years old. It seems to be locally known as "the BEAVERS." Its sign is a pictorial one with the arms duly displayed. Larwood and Hotten describe the GENERAL'S ARMS at Little Baddow as a "new-fangled, unmeaning sign," through knowing nothing of its local significance. It appears that the house belongs to Lord Rayleigh, and the arms of the Strutt family—crest, motto, and all—are correctly depicted upon the sign-board. It takes its name from Major-General William Goodday Strutt, brother of the first Baron. After seeing much active service, in which he lost a leg and received many wounds, he was appointed Governor of Quebec, and died February 5, 1848.

The ROYAL ARMS are displayed in the undesirable neighbourhood of Silvertown. Although our present Queen has now reigned fifty years, the QUEEN'S ARMS only appear three times on Essex sign-boards, against no less than seventeen KING'S ARMS. Probably the fact that the number of kings has been very much greater than the number of queens will fully account for this. There is, however, a VICTORIA ARMS at Brentwood. It seems probable that during the last forty years many houses formerly known as the KING'S HEAD have come to be called the KING'S ARMS, after the recent craze for "arms;" for the former sign was much commoner, and the latter much rarer, forty years since than now. It may be pointed out, for instance, that in Mr. Creed's list of signs round Epping in 1789, the King's *Head* appears six times, and the King's *Arms* only once; also that the Queen's *Head* appears twice, while the Queen's *Arms* does not appear at all. This shows the great prevalence of "Heads" over "Arms" on the signboards of last century, and also that the present prevalence of *Kings* over *Queens* in the same situation was observable even then. Probably the two Queen's Heads given, which were at Harlow and Fyfield respectively, represented the portrait of Queen Anne. A token was issued by William Drane at the KING'S ARMS (depicted in the field), in Waltham Abbey in 1668, and the same sign is mentioned in the

Chelmsford Chronicle for 1786 as occurring at Halstead. The sign still exists at both those places; but it is, of course, difficult to say whether or not the houses are the same as those that displayed the sign in the seventeenth and eighteenth centuries respectively. The sign of the KING'S ARMS at Waltham Abbey in 1668 can hardly have been more than eight years old at the time, as no one would have ventured to display such a sign during the time of the Commonwealth. Doubtless it was set up at the time of the Restoration in 1660 in honour of the new king, Charles II., for whose father, perhaps, this William Drane had fought.

Among the more miscellaneous " Arms " may be mentioned the CHATSWORTH ARMS at Forest Gate, the ALMA ARMS (beer-house) at Navestock, the CHOBHAM ARMS at Stratford, together with a LIBERTY ARMS, a LIBRA ARMS, three ORDNANCE ARMS, a RAILWAY ARMS, and a ROMAN ARMS in the Roman Road, Colchester. The last-named sign has been corrupted within the last twenty years from the ROMAN URN. Most of these extremely absurd signs have come into existence during the last few years. They serve to show how completely the original use of arms as signs has become disassociated from their present use. Another indication of the modern growth of " Arms " is to be found in the fact that they are very common as beer-house signs—beer-houses having only been instituted since the beginning of this century. Even forty years ago " Arms " were decidedly less common as signs than they are now. The list has of late been swelled by such stupid and unmeaning additions as the ALMA ARMS, LIBRA ARMS, and LILLIPUT ARMS, very few, if any, of which existed fifty years since.

To the above may be added the following, which appear in London, and are most of them modern and meaningless absurdities :—The WATERLOO ARMS, the GRAND JUNCTION ARMS, the PAVIORS' ARMS, the PALACE ARMS, the ROMAN ARMS (in the Roman Road, Bow, E.), the MECHANICS' ARMS, and the VOLUNTEERS' ARMS. The SOL'S ARMS, in the Hampstead Road, commemorated by Dickens in *Bleak House*, still exists under the same name. " Arms " in London are very frequently situated in streets of the same name, and these streets are usually named after persons, who, it may be presumed, own property in them. Altogether there are in London no less than 352 distinct signs consisting of " Arms " of some kind or other, not counting the number of times each particular sign is repeated. Thus, in London, "Arms" form rather more than twenty per cent. of all distinct signs.

CHAPTER III.

MAMMALIAN SIGNS.

HE next great class of signs to be noticed consists of what may be termed " Mammalian Signs." In Essex no less than 464 houses, or 34·2 per cent. of the whole, display devices derived from the animal kingdom. There are, however, only 102 distinct signs. These may be classified as follows:—

	No. of signs.	No. of distinct signs.
Mammals	384	81
Birds	75	18
Fish	1	1
Insects	4	2
	464	102

This calculation is, moreover, made independent of " man and his parts," as the heralds say. Signs of human origin have been placed in a separate class, and will be treated of hereafter by themselves.

Although many of the signs belonging to this class are, undoubtedly, nothing more than very modern vulgarisms, there can be no doubt whatever that a great number have a truly heraldic origin, as will be seen from what follows.

To commence the list, we find at Buckhurst Hill a BALD-FACED STAG, and in the adjoining parish of Chigwell a BALD HIND. These two signs have, doubtless, the same origin, but one which it is not now easy to discover. In Essex a horse is always said to be " bald " when he has a white face.

Possibly the signs commemorate the killing of two deer with white faces in the adjoining forest, which was the last locality in the east or south-east of England in which the aboriginal wild red deer survived, the last having been killed so lately as the year 1817 or thereabouts. Both the BALD HIND and the BALD-FACED STAG are among the oldest of the forest inns. The latter is, presumably, the same house marked as the BALD STAG on Cary's map, published in 1768. It has the same name in Mr. Creed's list (p. 7). The Rev. Wm. Cole tells us, in his voluminous MSS., that

BALD-FACED STAG.
(*Buckhurst Hill.*)

on the morning of October 27, 1774, he "started from the COCK at Epping without eating, and breakfasted at an Inne, called the BALD-FACED STAG." The existing inn is a large square, white-washed building, with a high-pitched roof. It contains a portrait of Queen Anne, and the coffee-room is panelled. From it, according to the author of *Nooks and Corners in Essex* (p. 21), the famous "Epping Hunt," so cleverly satirized by Tom Hood, used to start every Easter Monday, when it was no uncommon thing for five hundred mounts to ride off from the ridge on which the house stands. The Easter Monday hunt is said to have originated as far back as the year 1226, in the reign of Henry III. The custom was kept up until so recent a date as 1853, after which it gradually fell off, owing to the rough East End element which marked the annual meeting, and made it little more than a public nuisance. The stag—a tame one —was, on these occasions, taken round in turn to all the neighbouring public-houses before being set at liberty, and the amount of liquor consumed, and riot occasioned, was, in consequence, considerable. Something approaching a cele-

ROEBUCK.
(*Buckhurst Hill.*)

bration of the old custom has, however, been attempted as lately as the last two or three years. There was also a BALD-FACED STAG at Hatfield Broad Oak in 1789.

At Buckhurst Hill there is also a ROEBUCK, as well as a REINDEER. The former is marked on Cary's map, published in 1768, and is probably the same house several times spoken of (p. 6) as the BUCK in *The Trials of John Swan and Elizabeth Jeffries*, published in 1752. It is still one of the best and most widely-known inns on the Forest. In its large Assembly Room public gatherings often take place. The old REINDEER, which is shown on Cary's map, published in 1768, is now a private house, inhabited by Captain

Mackenzie, the Forest Superintendent, and known as
"Warren House." The present REINDEER is situated
about a mile distant from the old one. An ARCHER SHOOT-
ING AT A STAG is also depicted on the undated halfpenny
token of "John Unwin at Layton Stone."

It is in every way probable that the fallow deer, formerly
living in the surrounding forests of Epping and Hainault,
and still existing in considerable numbers in the former,
gave rise in some way to these numerous cervine signs in
and around the parish of Buckhurst Hill. It is, however,
a moot point whence the parish derived its name. Some
connect the name with Lord Buckhurst, a favourite of Queen
Elizabeth; others regard it as composed of two Anglo-Saxon
words, *Boc*, a beech, and *hurst*, a wood or forest, which is not
unlikely to be the true derivation; others, however, state
that this part of the forest was severed from the remainder
by Royal Charter, and so termed Book-hurst, meaning book-
forest; while yet others consider the name to mean Buckhurst, the wood or forest in which bucks lived. The latter
derivation seems in every way the most likely one. Nevertheless, the place was formerly often called "Buckit's Hill,"
as, for instance, in *The Trial of John Swan and Elizabeth
Jeffries* (p. 8), published in 1752, but this was probably a
corruption. The farthing of "William Locken in Tollsbvry
in Esex, 1668," bore a STAG, and that of "John Attewell in
Black Notle in Esex, 1670," bore THREE STAGS' HEADS
couped, probably taken from the coat of arms of some private
family. The STAG'S HEAD at Colchester is also, probably, a
form of some family crest. Forty years ago there was a
DOE INN at Halstead. There is now a STAG at Hatfield
Heath, and another at Little Easton. Concerning the
latter, there can be very little doubt that it represents the
crest of the Maynard family (*a stag statant or*). It would be
interesting to learn whether this house has come to be known
as the STAG after having first been called the MAYNARD ARMS.
The STAG also serves as a beer-house sign at High Ongar.
It is not very easy to say what first led to the REINDEER
being used as a sign; but that it was in use as early as the

seventeenth century is clear from what Pepys says in his *Diary*.
He tells us that on the night of October 7, 1667, he "lay
very well" at the "Rayne-deere at Bishop Stafford" (meaning
Bishops Stortford), where the sign is still in existence. The
same sign also occurs at Takeley, Black Notley, and (as
already mentioned) Buckhurst Hill, having been probably
set up at the latter place in order to keep company with the
other kinds of deer that are found there. The REINDEER at
Takeley has been in existence since 1786 at least, as it is
mentioned in the *Chelmsford Chronicle* on January 20th in that

CROWN HOUSE.
(*Newport, Essex.*)

year. At Greenstead, near Colchester, there is to be seen
the sign of the BUCK'S HORNS, which is very likely intended
to represent the deer's "*attires*" in somebody's coat of arms.
The sign is not mentioned by Larwood and Hotten. The
HORNS at Barking Side may have had the same origin, or
the house may have taken its sign from the noted tavern of
the same name which formerly existed in Fleet Street. The
residence at Newport, now commonly known as the Crown
House (from the crown sculptured over the door), or Nell
Gwynne's House, used formerly to be an inn. Its present

names have been given to it within living memory. Mr. C. K. Probert states [1] that in the time of his father, eighty or ninety years ago, there was a tradition still lingering in the town that the inn was formerly known as the HORNS, and that Charles II., The Duke of York, and Nell Gwynne used to stop there on their way from London to Newmarket races. This circumstance is alluded to in an old folio history of the Rye House Plot, and Mr. Probert has seen a play, printed about seventy years ago, in which the scene was laid at the HORNS at Newport, the characters being Charles II., Nell Gwynne, the Duke of York, &c. Mr. Probert writes:

"Tradition says they used to come with packhorses by the Great North Road, *viâ* Rickling and the lane near Wicken Bonhunt, still called 'London Lane;' then along the ancient road at the foot of Bury Field in Newport; then along the back of the Burywater House, and so emerging opposite the Crown House."

The HORN Hotel in the High Street at Braintree is a well-known old coaching inn, and has long been one of the best in the town. If the late Mr. Joseph Strutt is to be believed, this house, at the beginning of the present century, was known as the BUGLE HORN. In his Essex and Herts romance, entitled *Queenhoo Hall*, published in 1808, the hero relates (ii. p. 180) that "we took some dinner at the Bugle Horn at Braintree, and proceeded in the afternoon to Dunmow, where we arrived before sunset." In any case, this sign, like that of the HORN AND HORSESHOES at Harlow Common, is probably connected with the old coaching days. The sound of the horn and of the horses' shoes would be the first intimation of the approach of a stage-coach. The latter sign, however, may have some heraldic significance, as Larwood and Hotten mention a London token of 1666 on which a horseshoe is represented within a pair of antlers or *deer's attires*. In 1789, too, it seems to have been the HORNS AND HORSESHOES. The BUGLE HORN might easily be connected either with coaching, hunting, or heraldry, were it not situated in Barrack Street, *Colchester. This, of course, makes it in every way probable that it is a military sign. Here, also, must be noticed the popular sign of

[1] *Trans. Essex Arch. Soc.*, vol. v. p. 77.

the WHITE HART. This device appears to be unusually common in the county of Essex. Nearly every town or village of any consequence possesses an example. At present we have no less than fifty, and twenty years ago the number was exactly the same. London itself cannot boast of having more, as it has also just fifty examples of the sign. The WHITE HART in the High Street at Brentwood is in all respects the most notable house now displaying this sign in Essex. In its best days it was a coaching inn of great importance, and is still by far the best hotel in the town. Mr. H. W. King has ascertained that it was in existence under its present name in the time of Queen Elizabeth ; but, looking at the house itself, he believes it to be of still earlier date, perhaps of the fifteenth century, or even earlier. It is certainly one of the very best examples of an old-fashioned inn, with a central courtyard and galleries running round it, now remaining in England. It is mentioned in the *Chelms-ford Chronicle* for September 14, 1764, as a stopping-place for the coaches " which set out on Monday the 27th instant at 7 o'clock in the morning from the Black Bull in Bishops-gate, London, and at the same time from the Great White Horse Inn [1] in Ipswich, and continue every day (Sunday excepted) to be at the above places the same evening at 5 o'clock. Each passenger to pay 3 pence per mile and to be allowed 18 pounds luggage," &c.

During the reign of Elizabeth the WHITE HART was also the principal inn in the town of Saffron Walden, but it is not now known in what street the house was situated. Possibly the inn now known as the HOOPS, in King Street, was the WHITE HART of those days, as it is a very ancient structure. Boyne describes a farthing bearing the GROCERS' ARMS, and issued by " Anne Mathews, in Safforn Walden, 1656." Mr. H. Ecroyd Smith has ascertained, from the registers in the church, that a few years later she married John Potter of the WHITE HART, and also that they thereupon jointly issued fresh tokens, retaining her name, arms, and date on the obverse, but having a new reverse, bearing the words " John

[1] A once-famous coaching house mentioned by Dickens in *Pickwick.*

Potter," and in the centre a *hart lodged* with the monogram " I.A.P." over it, perhaps to indicate that they continued to carry on their two trades simultaneously. On the 25th of February, 1659, Pepys says in his *Diary* : " Mr. Blayton and I took horse, and straight to Saffron Walden, where, at the White Hart, we set up our horses, and took the master of the house [in all probability the aforesaid John Potter] to show us Audly End House." References to this inn occur early on in the records of the Corporation of Walden. Thus, in 1627, 14s. was expended " for wine when the Earl of Sussex was at the White Hart ; " in 1631, 9s. was " spent at the White Hart when we ourselves did ring for the king ; " in 1643, 2s. 10d. was " payd at the White Hart when Radcliffe was taken for a Jesuit ; " and in 1661, the sum of 3s. 4d. was " spent at the White Hart when the ryot was, some of the company being there." The WHITE HART on a sign-board at Boreham is correctly and heraldically represented, but has evidently, in the mind of the artist, been associated with the deer in Boreham Park, as a view of Boreham House has been introduced in the background. The WHITE HART at Great Yeldham is a very ancient village hostel. Its windows, and its exterior generally, are quaint and antique. In front of the inn, on each side of the door, are old oaken settles, whereon the village sages debate the topics of the day. From the sign-board on the Green opposite, the white hart has long since departed. The WHITE HART in Tindal Street, *Chelmsford, has a new and large graven sign, heraldically represented, and prominently projected over the street. The WHITE HART at *Witham, too, has a large and rather grotesque sign, though it is correctly represented. It is rudely cut out of what appears to be a thin sheet of iron, and is suspended over the pavement. The WHITE HART at *Coggeshall—doubtless the existing hotel—is mentioned in *Bufton's Diary* in 1678.[1] It is also recorded in *Bufton's Diary*[2] that " In April, 1682, there was ye floore of a Chamber fell downey at ye WHITE HART at Bocking [probably the still existing Hotel of that

---

[1] Dale's *Annals of Coggeshall*, p. 261.   [2] Ibid. p. 265.

name], where ye Justices sat and about 200 people in ye roome, and one man broke his leg." In an early number of the *Gentleman's Magazine* is an illustration of an old inscribed beam from the WHITE HART between Springfield and Boreham. Mr. J. A. Repton in a note says that the building was thought to have been a hermitage. He adds: "There is a long inscription at the bottom of one of the gables, but it is at present concealed with plaster;" "that the beam measured 52 inches by seven; and that it bore the inscription, ' Jesus! Mercy! Lady help! Jesus!'" Taylor, in his *Catalogue of Tavernes*, mentions a WHITE HART at *Romford in 1636, probably the hotel of that name still existing there. An inn with this sign at Colchester is mentioned in one of the old Corporation records, dated 1603, as being an "auncyent inne" at that time. In old deeds Mr. H. W. King finds mention of a WHITE HART—either inn, shop, or tenement—at Horndon-on-the-Hill in both 1704 and 1719. There does not seem to be any apparent reason why the white hart should have become so common a device as a sign as it has done. According to Larwood and Hotten, its use dates from a very remote period; but there can be very little doubt that its present abundance is due to the fact that *a White Hart lodged, collared and chained or*, was the favourite badge of King Richard II., and appears, with variations, no less than eighty-three times upon his monument at Westminster. At a tournament held in Smithfield in 1390, in honour of various foreign counts who had been elected members of the garter—

" All the kynges house were of one sute ; theyr cotys, theyr armys, theyr sheldes, and theyr trappours were bowdrid all with whyte hertys, with crownes of gold about their neck, and cheyns of gold hanging thereon, which hertys was the kinges leverye that he gaf to lordes, ladyes, knyghtes and squyers, to know his household people from others."

The White Hart was also used as a badge by Edward IV. It is just possible that the fact of the crest of the Maynard family being a stag, as already mentioned, has something to do with the abundance of the WHITE HART as a sign in Essex, or at least in the northern parts of the county. It is

possible, too, that the abundance of this sign in Essex may
be due in part to the fact that a very ancient and famous
WHITE HART formerly stood in Bishopsgate Street Without,
in such a position that it would probably form a stopping-
place for most travellers to and from London along the Great
East Road. Timbs, in his *Clubs and Club-life in London*
(p. 397), says that it was originally built in 1480, but the old
house was pulled down and rebuilt in modern style in 1829.
Allusion has already been made (p. 25) to an absurd corruption of this sign at West Bergholt, where the landlord of the
WHITE HART, not content with a script sign, has added a

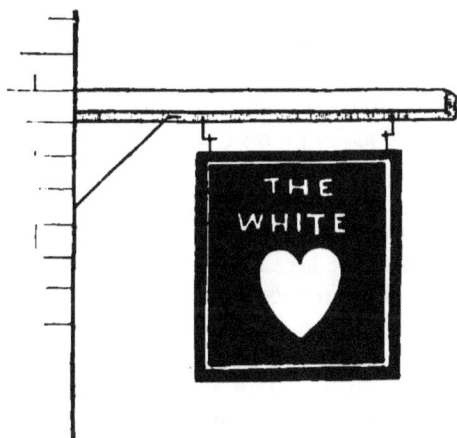

THE WHITE HART (Heart).
(*At West Bergholt.*)

THE WHITE HART.

pictorial one of his own designing, representing a large
WHITE HEART on a black ground! Whether this has been
done through ignorance or intent, it is a good example of the
way signs become corrupted and altered in the course of time.
Illustrations of both forms are given above.

The horse and his belongings are referred to no less than
seventy-three times on Essex sign-boards, although a simple
horse does not once occur. The use of the horse as a sign
is probably derived both from the animal himself and from the
part he anciently played in Heraldry. Horses of fantastic

colour, such as the GOLDEN HORSE at Forest Gate, are, in all probability, of heraldic origin. No less than thirty-six times in this county do we meet with the sign of the WHITE HORSE, and there is an OLD WHITE HORSE at North Ockendon. Boyne describes tokens issued by " John Tvrner at the White Horse in Chelmsford, 1667," and by " John Langston at the Whit Horse in Mvchboddow." WHITE HORSES are still in existence at both of these places. There can be no doubt that the one at Great Baddow is the one from which the token was issued in the seventeenth century ; but in the case of Chelmsford there is some doubt. The matter is not without interest, for there is in the British Museum a scarce and curious quarto tract, of twenty-one pages, published in the year 1688, with the following title : *A True Relation of a Horrid Murder, committed upon the person of Thomas Kidderminster of Tupsley in the County of Hereford, Gent., at the White Horse Inn in Chelmsford, in the County of Essex, in the Month of April, 1654, together with a True Account of the Strange and Providential Discovery of the Same nine years after, &c., &c.*" In this tract one Mr. Turner (without doubt the man who issued the token in 1667) is many times mentioned as landlord at the time the murder was discovered. Forty years ago the WHITE HORSE at Dovercourt styled itself the GREAT WHITE HORSE. The WHITE HORSE in the High Street, Maldon, is several times referred to in advertisements in the *Chelmsford Chronicle* during the year 1786. Likely origins for this sign have already been given (p. 18). The FLYING DUTCHMAN, which is a beer-house sign at Braintree, probably commemorates the racehorse of that name. There are BLACK HORSES at White Roothing, Widdington, Sible Hedingham, Pilgrim's Hatch, and Chelmsford (beerhouse). Sixty years ago there was another at *Coggeshall. There are also YORKSHIRE GREYS at Coggeshall (at least forty years old), Stratford (two), and Brentwood. Probably these are named after some famous racer. One or other of those at *Stratford is several times referred to in the *Trials of John Swan and Elizabeth Jeffries* (1752). It was then kept by a certain Ann Wright. Sixty years since, too, there was another at *Colchester. Adjoining the racecourse at Galleywood there is a RUNNING MARE. The NAG'S HEAD is a sign which seems to be becoming increasingly common, as we have five now existing in the county, not counting a beer-house so called at Chelmsford, though, twenty years ago, there were only three. The sign of the THREE COLTS, which occurs at Stanstead Montfitchet and Buckhurst Hill, has very likely an heraldic origin. It is not a modern device, as there was an inn of this name in Bride Lane, London, in 1652, and our houses may have taken their name from this one. A HORSE *passant* is depicted on the farthing token of " Ioseph Gleson," 1664, and a HORSE GALLOPING on that of " Samvell Salter," 1656, both of Dedham. In Essex the horse enters into many combinations with other sign-board objects. In most cases the meaning of the combination is so evident that no explanation of it is required. For instance, at Colchester we find a CHAISE AND PAIR, at Stratford a CART AND HORSES, at Mistley a WAGGON AND HORSES, and another at *Colchester. There are also beer-houses so called at Braintree and Hadleigh. The COACH AND HORSES occurs no less than thirteen times, the OLD COACH AND HORSES once, the HORSE AND GROOM seven times, and the HORSE AND WHEEL once. This latter is, however, a misprint on the part of the compilers of the *Post Office Directory.* Twenty years ago it appeared in the list as the HORSE AND WELL, and as the house is situated at Woodford Wells, this is undoubtedly its correct form. The sign is not mentioned by Larwood and Hotten. That part of Woodford known as Woodford Wells, takes its name from a mineral spring which once existed there. It was formerly in great repute, but is now quite dry and neglected. An *Itinerary of Twenty-five Miles round London,* published towards the end of last century, and quoted by Mr. Walford in *Greater London* (vol. i. p. 464), indicates that the name of the house was then the HORSE AND GROOM. The adjoining mineral spring, says the author, " was formerly in good repute, and much company resorted to drink the waters at a house of public entertainment called ' WOODFORD WELLS ; ' but the waters have long lost their reputation." Hood, in his witty poem on the Epping Hunt, refers to the house as follows:

> " Now many a sign at Woodford Town,
>   Its Inn-vitation tells ;
>   But Huggins, full of ills, of course,
>   Betook him to the WELLS."

The HORSE AND GROOM at Great Warley seems to be at least a century old, as it is mentioned in the *Chelmsford Chronicle* on March 10, 1786. At Margaret Roothing there is a HORSESHOE, which is a comparatively rare sign by itself. The BULL AND HORSESHOE at North Weald is, doubtless, merely an impaled sign. Our three HORSESHOES and ten THREE HORSESHOES have already been referred to (p. 40). At Finchingfield there is a beer-house with the sign of the KICKING DICKEY, and the CROSS KEYS at Roxwell is commonly known in the parish by the same name. The origin of the sign, which Larwood and Hotten do not mention, is hard to explain.

The Lion, with frequent variations of colour and position, is of common occurrence in the county. This great variety in colouring clearly shows that we are indebted to the art of Heraldry for most of our sign-board lions. Messrs. Larwood and Hotten say (p. 118): " The *lion rampant* most frequently occurs, although in late years naturalism has crept in, and the *Felis leo* is often represented standing or crouching, quite regardless of his heraldic origin."

When it is remembered that *three lions passant, guardant, or* occur on the Royal Arms of England, and a *lion rampant gules* on the arms of Scotland; that a *crowned lion statant, guardant or* is used as the Royal Crest of England, a *crowned lion sejant affrontée gules* as the Royal Crest of Scotland, and a *lion rampant guardant, or* as the dexter supporter of the Royal Arms of England; and that lions of various colours and in different attitudes have served as charges, badges, crests, and supporters to many of our earlier sovereigns, and now appear in the armorial bearings of innumerable private families, it will not be found in any way surprising that the lion figures so commonly as he does upon our sign-boards.

So frequently, indeed, are lions made use of in Heraldry that it is almost impossible to assign the variously-coloured examples now to be seen on our sign-boards to their original wearers. *Lions rampant* appear on the trade-tokens of John Rayment of Brentwood, in 1669, and of Richard Boyse and Richard Rich, both of Colchester, in 1668 and 1656 respectively. At present the animal occurs eight times in Essex as a simple LION, and once as a BRITISH LION. The LION at Chelmsford, although it has now disappeared, was once evidently a very important inn. The Rev. R. E. Bartlett finds several mentions of it in the parish registers, the earliest before the middle of the sixteenth century. They are as follows: " 1543. William Knight, a stranger, who by misfortune and his own lewdness was drowned at the Lion, and was buried the 22nd of May." Again, in 1545, " Wyllyam Pemberton, servaunte to the Irle of Essex, was slayne at the Lion by one of his Fellows and bury'd the 19th Day of Januarii." From the first of these it appears that the inn was near the river. Taylor, in his *Catalogue of Tavernes*, also mentions the LION as one of the chief inns in Chelmsford in 1636. Whether this was the same inn afterwards known as the WHITE LION, and mentioned in the *Chelmsford Chronicle* on April 14, 1786, as then existing at Chelmsford, is hard to say. Possibly the latter house was identical with that shown with the sign of a rampant lion in the frontispiece. Its back premises would probably abut upon the river bank. The site is now occupied by an inn with the sign of the QUEEN'S ARMS. The GOLDEN LION, if it does not represent the true "lion of England," may represent the *lion passant, guardant, or* which appears on the arms of the Haberdashers' Company.[1] The sign now occurs at Prittlewell, *Chelmsford, *Romford, and Rayleigh. There are also beer-shops so-called at Braintree, Hatfield Peverell, Rochford, and elsewhere. The GOLDEN LION at Rayleigh is mentioned in the *Chelmsford Chronicle* for February 24, 1786. Sixty years ago another house of

---

[1] Barry nebulée of six, argent and azure ; on a bend gules, a lion passant guardant or.

this name existed. A GOLDEN LION at Harwich in 1764 is also mentioned in the *Chelmsford Chronicle* for that year. The sign of the BLUE LION occurs at Galleywood and at Great Baddow. Larwood and Hotten think that it "may possibly have been first put up at the marriage of James I. with Anne of Denmark." There can, however, be very little doubt that in Essex this sign represents the arms of the Mildmay family,[1] which was once of very great influence in the county. At the time of James I. there were nine several families of this name possessed of very large estates in the county, the heads of eight of them being knights. Our nine WHITE LIONS perhaps represent the badge of Edward IV., though the Dukes of Norfolk, the Earls of Surrey, and other prominent personages have also borne *lions argent*. Forty years since an OLD WHITE LION existed at Epping, being probably the *WHITE LION which lived there in 1789 (p. 7). As he has now disappeared, it is only natural to suppose that he has died of old age. The sign-board of the existing house at Epping is fully pictorial. The WHITE LION at Waltham Abbey is mentioned in the parish registers in July, 1746, when W. Chesson (presumably the landlord) was buried. BLACK LIONS are to be seen at Plaistow, Stisted, Althorne, Layer Marney, High Roothing, and *Epping. At the last-mentioned place two houses of this name existed forty years ago, one of which has existed since 1789, at least. According to advertisements in the issues of the *Chelmsford Chronicle* for February 10 and April 14, 1786, a BLACK LION then existed at Braintree; but, unless identical with the LION AND LAMB or WHITE LION, still in existence there, it has now disappeared. Larwood and Hotten say (p. 120), "The BLACK LION is somewhat uncommon; it may have been derived from the coat of arms of Queen Philippa of Hainault, wife of Edward III.," or it may represent the *lion sable* in the arms of Owen Glendower. The RED LION is, however, by far our commonest leonine sign in Essex. It occurs as many as thirty-four times. The authors

---

[1] Argent; three lions rampant azure, armed and langued gules. Crest and supporters, the same device in different positions.

so frequently quoted, say (p. 119) that it doubtless originated in the badge of John of Gaunt, Duke of Lancaster,
who bore the lion of Leon and Castille on his arms as a
token of his claim to the throne of those countries. In after
years it may often have been used to represent the lion of
Scotland. The RED LION, opposite the church at Stambourne, has a truly heraldic sign—*a lion, rampant, gules,
armed, langued, &c., argent, on a wreath argent and sable.* On
one of its gables this inn has two designs—one representing
an old man with long white hair, wearing a large green coat
and boots of the same colour, and apparently blowing a long
horn or trumpet; the other a monogram " I.W.E." and the
date 1709. This may indicate that it was formerly known as
the GREEN MAN. The RED LION at *Colchester is a very
well-known house. Like the WHITE HART at Brentwood, it is
one of the few examples now remaining in the county of the
old-fashioned inn of several centuries ago. Its capacious
courtyard has evidently once been galleried, and it is altogether one of the most ancient inns now existing in Colchester, or even in the county, as well as being certainly one
of the most quaint and antique in its appearance. Its upper-
most story considerably overhangs the others, and the whole
of the front shows much old carving which is certainly not
later than the fifteenth, and probably the fourteenth, century,
to which has been added some good modern work. Probably
if the plaster were removed much more old carving would be
brought to light. Among other faces, are those of two lions,
which look down upon the entrance. The doorway is also
carved. Miss L. S. Costello, in an article on Colchester in
Bentley's Miscellany for 1840 (vol. xviii. p. 62), says, that among
the few interesting houses in the High Street, she " was
struck with a wooden doorway at the entrance of the [RED]
LION INN. It has evidently been elaborately carved on the
different storeys all over, but very little of its ornament
remains. The spandrels of the arch have a representation,
on one side, of a dragon, huge and grim, and on the other
of a knight on foot, with an immensely long spear, tilting at
the monster." An entry, dated Jan. 9, 1603–4, in one of

the old Corporation assembly books, states that "the Lion, the Angel, and the White Hart were appointed the only three wine taverns in yᵉ towne, being auncyent Innes and Taverns." Mr. Chas. Golding of Colchester has, however, traced its existence back many years earlier, having found mention of it under its present name in the Corporation records of the year 1530 or thereabouts. The still-extant RED LIONS at Great Wakering and Ilford are referred to in advertisements in the *Chelmsford Chronicle* on Jan. 20 and 27, 1786, respectively. The latter was a posting-house of great importance in the days when coaching was at its height ; but, like its neighbour, the ANGEL (another house once of considerable fame), it has now sunk into comparative insignificance, though still quite one of the leading inns of the district. It is a large, massive square brick building, before which on the top of the sign-post reposes a graven representation of a Red Lion *couchant*. The RED LION at Waltham Abbey is referred to in the parish registers in 1644, when 1s. 8d. was "given to the woman that lay in at the Reed Lyon." Capt. Andrew Hamilton has given [1] an interesting account of an old house at Kelvedon, formerly known as the RED LION Inn. It is now converted into four good-sized tenements, and is known as Knight Templars Terrace, from a tradition that the inn once belonged to that fraternity. In its day it was probably the most considerable inn in Kelvedon, and the largest on the main road between Chelmsford and Colchester. It was certainly built before the year 1420, and is now an excellent example of a half-timbered house of that date. Until lately, however, the original work has been hidden by no less than two false fronts of lath and plaster of the seventeenth and eighteenth centuries respectively. Capt. Hamilton describes in detail both the internal and external construction of this singularly interesting house, but his remarks are too lengthy to quote here. Opposite to it stood the ANGEL.

The RED LION at Abberton figures in the Rev. S. Baring-Gould's *Mehalah*. The RED LION at Springfield is

[1] *Trans. Essex Arch. Soc.*, N. S., vol. i. p. 153.

an extremely ferocious one, if one may judge from the appearance of his effigy, which is rudely cut out of a thin sheet of iron, painted red, and placed upon the top of the beer-house to which he serves as a sign. A RED LION at Radwinter (perhaps the existing LION) finds mention in the *Chelmsford Chronicle* on January 20, 1786. The LION AND BOAR at Earls Colne may represent the lion and boar which sometimes appear as the supporters of the arms of King Richard III., or it may simply be an impaled sign. The sign is not mentioned by Larwood and Hotten. The LION AND KEY at Leyton is a sign of somewhat obscure origin. It is not a modern invention, as there was a house of the same name near Lion's Quay, London, in 1653. Our house, which is over forty years old, and was formerly a blacksmith's shop, may have taken its sign from this one, or it may have derived its name independently from the popular version of some family crest. This is rendered extremely likely from the fact (supplied by the present landlord, who, however, is unable to give any further information as to the sign) that among the old property taken with the house is a punch-bowl bearing the heraldic device of a lion rampant, its paw resting upon the ring of an upright key, and dated either 1756 or 1786. Whose this crest is, it is hard to say. The Rev. H. L. Elliot has ascertained that it is not included among those in *The Book of Family Crests*, although the family of Lyngard of Northants bore *a lion sejant guardant sable, in the dexter fore paw a key in pale or;* while the families of Knox, Criall, and Chamberlain had crests with a demi-lion holding a key. The very common sign of the LION AND LAMB is now met with at Braintree, Stratford, Takeley, Chelmsford, and Brentwood, although, twenty years ago, the county only contained three examples. At the last-named place the sign seems to have existed since 1786 at least, as it is mentioned in the *Chelmsford Chronicle* on March 17th in that year. At *Chelmsford a LION AND LAMB carved in stone repose peacefully upon the parapet of the building, while a newly-painted sign-board, very well designed, depicts them in the same attitude. The fact of the name containing an alliteration has, no doubt, had something to do with its adoption ; but it is also an emblematic representation of the Millennium, when (as Larwood and Hotten say) " the lion shall lie down by the kid." Those gentlemen, however, together with all who use the sign, appear to be a little at fault in their knowledge of Scripture. The passage describing the " Millennium " (Isaiah xi. 6) says nothing about a lion lying down, either with a lamb or a kid. It runs as follows: " The wolf shall dwell with the lamb, and the leopard shall lie down with the kid ; and the calf and the young lion and the fatling together." The sign first came into use over two centuries ago. In connection with this sign there is an amusing tale, which is worth repeating, told of a sceptical American. When the significance of the sign was explained to him, he remarked that the state of things depicted might possibly come to pass some time, but that, when it did, he "guessed that there Lamb would be inside that there Lion!"

Bovine signs are very frequently to be seen upon our Essex sign-boards. The simple sign of the BULL is the commonest device, occurring no less than twenty-two times. Its intimate connection with Christmas beef, heraldry, and bull-baiting is sufficient to account for the frequent appearance of this animal on the sign-board. About seventy years ago the BULL Inn, Whitechapel, was the resort of the Essex farmers, who came to London once a week to dispose of their corn, &c. The landlord, named Johnson, who was formerly "boots" at this inn, being in good credit with his customers, they occasionally left their samples with him, and he acted as a middle man so much to their satisfaction, that he shortly after opened an office upon Bear Quay, styling himself " Factor of the Essex Farmers." The business ultimately grew to one of great extent. In old deeds Mr. King finds mention of a BULL—either shop, inn, or dwelling-house—at Billericay as early as 1616, also of another house with the same sign at Hockley early in the seventeenth century. Taylor, in his *Catalogue of Tavernes,* mentions a BULL (probably the existing inn of that name) at Barking in 1636, and another at Brook Street, where also there is a still existing Bull.

The BLACK BULL appears at Fyfield, Chelmsford, Margaretting, and Old Sampford, while an OLD BLACK BULL occurs at Stratford. Very probably these two signs owe their existence to the fact that a *bull sable* formed one of the badges, as well as the sinister supporter of the arms, of Edward IV. In 1662 there was a BLACK BULL Inn at Romford, as appears from a mention made of it in the *Account of the Murder of Thomas Kidderminster*, already referred to. In 1789 there were other examples of the BLACK BULL at Loughton and Harlow, and that at Fyfield was then existing. Sixty years ago there was also one at Grays. On the map of the road between London and Harwich, given in Ogilby's *Itinerarium Angliæ*, published in 1675, " Ye BULL INN " —evidently a house of some importance—is shown about midway between Ingatestone and Widford. In the *Traveller's Guide*, a smaller edition of the same work, published in 1699, the same house figures as the BLACK BULL Inn. Probably this is the still existing BLACK BULL at Margaretting. The BULL AND CROWN, which has been in existence at Chingford for at least forty years past, may be simply an impaled sign, or it may (like the last sign spoken of) be derived from the black bull of Edward IV., or from the white bull used as a supporter by Henry VIII. In either case the bull would probably be crowned. This device is not referred to in the *History of Sign-boards*, nor is that of the BULL AND HORSESHOE, which occurs at North Weald. It is probably only an impaled sign. The BULL'S HEAD, to be seen at Loughton, is, as already stated (p. 34), probably taken from the arms of the Butchers' Company. There was once a famous BULL Inn at Newport. It has now disappeared, having, it is said, been compelled to close owing to the opening of the HERCULES just opposite; but there are old folks still living who can recollect the shields of arms in coloured glass in the windows, and the " Bull Orchard " still remains. The house is mentioned in the Corporation records of Saffron Walden for the year 1734. Cole also, in his MSS., speaks of it by the name of the RED BULL (a rather uncommon sign, of which Essex does not now possess an example). The sign, however, seems to have undergone a change of colour, for it is referred to as the BLACK BULL in *Poor Robin's Perambulation from Saffron Walden to London, performed this month of July*, 1678.[1] The author says :

> "To Newport Pond my course I next way bent,
> And in at the sign of the Black Bull went.
> Where scarcely in a room I had set down,
> When in came my old friends, kind Mr. Br . . .
> And Mr. Woo . . . ., two who love their friend
> With true and hearty love unto the end ;
> For though they in another town do live,
> They to their neighbour some kind visits give.
> 'Twas twelve o'clock ; dinner time did approach,
> When men whet knives on wheels of cart or coach.
> The cloth was laid, and by the scent o' th' meat,
> One might perceive there something was to eat.
> And so it proved, indeed ; for from the pot
> Came forth a rump of beef, was piping hot,
> And from the spit was brought a loyn of mutton,
> Would satisfy the stomack of a glutton,
> For like a loyn of beef it might well have been knighted,
> To which our hostess kindly us invited ;
> Which we accepted of, and to delight her,
> Told her that none could deny such an inviter ;
> For she's a widow of such excellent carriage,
> Would make a man most happy in her marriage," &c.

Boyne describes a halfpenny token issued by "Thomas Rvnham at yᵉ Bull [represented in the centre] in Newport, 1667." He assigns the token to Newport in Shropshire; but, as Mr. Joseph Clarke, F.S.A., has informed the author that no less than seven examples have been found at Newport, Essex, and as the man's name also occurs in the parish register, there can be no doubt that Boyne was wrong.[2] At Chingford Hatch there is a house with the sign of the DUN COW. This is an ancient device, and probably has reference to the feat of Guy, Earl of Warwick, who, according to an old ballad, slew a "dun cow bigger than an elephaunt" on Dunsmore Heath. The RED COW, as a sign, may be seen at Chrishall, Ashen, and Shelley. A once well-known RED COW at *Chelms-

---

[1] Only a single copy is now known to exist of this remarkable production of the effusive Walden poet and would-be wit, Robert Winstanley.

[2] It is interesting, too, to note that tokens are still in existence, inscribed " Henry Woodley, 1657, at Newport Pond, H. W." This, in all probability, was the " Mr. Woo . . . ." mentioned by Poor Robin.

ford is now an equally well-known coffee-tavern with the same sign. At Waltham Holy Cross a beer-shop displays the very strange sign of the Spotted Cow, which is in all probability unique. Larwood and Hotten do not mention it. The sign of the Red Cow is probably intended to express the idea that good drink may be obtained within, as from a cow ; but, in former times, especial value seems to have attached to the milk of red cows. At Cold Norton, near Maldon, there is a house with the very strange, and probably unique, sign of the Fly and Bullock, kept by one William Pond. It is at first difficult to see what possible sign-board connection the two creatures can have. Farmers have reasons for believing that, during hot weather, a great animosity exists between the two. Inquiry has at last elicited the fact that the sign is a corrupted one, but this was not arrived at until after much amusing and erudite speculation, as the sign in its present form is a very perplexing one. The first guess was that it was a corruption of the " Flying Bullock " or " Winged Bull," the usual emblem of St. Luke. This seemed the more likely, as we have in Essex signs which might represent at least two other of the Apostolic emblems, namely, the Angel for Matthew, and the Eagle for John ; and who can say but that some of our Lions were not once winged, thus representing the only remaining Evangelist, Mark ? Moreover, Larwood and Hotten, although they do not refer to this sign, mention (p. 73), when speaking of the sign of the Flying Horse, " a facetious innkeeper at Rogate, Petersfield, who has put up a parody in the shape of a *Flying Bull.*" But then arose the question, " Why should Luke be thus commemorated ? " It was next suggested in several quarters that the sign might have originated in the old fable of *La Mouche et le Toreau,* of which Miss Elliot of Gosfield has kindly forwarded a copy, and which is thought to be of Oriental origin. This, however, did not decide the question, so inquiry was made of the landlord, who, though knowing nothing of the origin of his sign, stated that it formerly was, and should now be, the Butchers' Arms, thereby clearing up the doubt, the crest and supporters of those arms being "Flying Bulls."[1]　There can be no doubt, therefore, that the FLY AND BULLOCK originally represented one of the FLYING BULLOCKS in the Butchers' Arms.　It seems, moreover, that the sign does after all represent the winged ox of St. Luke, that Evangelist being, in a way, the Patron Saint of butchers, for in Chambers's *Book of Days* (ii. p. 464) it is stated this symbol has been associated with St. Luke, "because, to quote the words of an ancient writer, ' he deviseth about the presthode of Jesus Christ,'· the ox or calf being the sign of a sacrifice, and St. Luke entering more largely than the other Evangelists into the history of the life and sufferings of our Saviour."

The BLUE BOAR is, perhaps, the most interesting of all our Essex signs.　At present it occurs five times in the county — namely, at *Prittlewell, *Maldon, *Colchester, *Stratford, and Abridge.　The two first-named houses have been in existence at least a century, as they are mentioned in advertisements in the *Chelmsford Chronicle* in 1786 and 1788 respectively, while the last-named is marked on Greenwood's Map of Essex, published in 1824.　Forty years ago there was another example of the sign at Stanford Rivers, and Mr. H. W. King informs the author that the house at Hadleigh, now known as the CASTLE, displayed the sign of the BLUE BOAR until late in the last century.　Taylor (see p. 28) mentions another BLUE BOAR at Ilford in 1636. In 1789, too, there was one at Fyfield.　In the year 1750, a BLUE BOAR'S HEAD Inn existed opposite the Church at Waltham Abbey.　Mr. Charles Golding, of Colchester, in writing to *Notes and Queries*[2] to inquire the latest date at which bull-baiting is known to have taken place in England, mentions that an entertainment of this kind was announced, in an old advertisement that he had seen, to take place at the above house on Whitsun Monday, 1750, and " any gentleman bringing a dog should be entertained at

---

[1] *Arms* (see p. 34).　*Crest:* On a wreath a Flying Bull argent, wings endorsed or, armed and hoofed of the last, over the head a small circle of glory, proper.　*Supporters:* Two Flying Bulls argent, winged, armed and hoofed or, over each head a small circle of glory, proper.

[2] Fifth Series, vol. xii. p. 328.

a dinner free." The same house is referred to in an entry in the parish registers in 1647, when 12s. 6d. was "paid for a dinner at the Borsehed when the ould Churchwardens gave up their accounts." The sign of the BOAR'S HEAD occurs at East Horndon, *Braintree, and *Dunmow. The first of these houses appeared in the list forty years ago as the OLD BOAR'S HEAD. Our houses of this name have, perhaps, been named after the famous BOAR'S HEAD tavern which used to exist in Eastcheap, or they may have had a separate origin. As to the derivation of the sign itself, Larwood and Hotten are inclined to believe that it represents the boar's head as formerly often brought to table, rather than a charge taken from some one's arms; but, in this, it is difficult altogether to agree with them. A boar's head forms part of the arms of the Butchers' Company (p. 34), and we have had in Essex several families bearing the same charge in their arms, such as the Borehams of Haverhill, the Welbores of Clavering, and the Tyrrells, Baronets, of Boreham House—the charge and the name of the place being very probably connected in some way in the latter case. Indeed, so far as the BOAR'S HEAD at East Horndon is concerned, there can be no doubt whatever that it represents the crest of the family of Tyrrells, Baronets (connected with the Boreham Tyrrells), formerly of Heron Hall, in the same parish, which was demolished about the year 1789. Their crest, which was *a boar's head, couped and erect, argent, issuant out of the mouth a peacock's tail proper*, is now correctly represented on the sign-board, exactly as upon several of the family monuments in the church. Both the sign-board and the heraldic device it bears are new, having been recently set up under the supervision of the rector of the parish. The old board, which is altogether unheraldic, is displayed over the door, and exhibits the head of an extremely ferocious-looking boar emerging from a clump of rushes in a most threatening manner.

There can be very little doubt that in Essex the sign of the BLUE BOAR represents the *boar azure, armed, unguled, and bristled or*, which served as a crest, as one of the supporters, and also as one of the principal badges of the once powerful De Veres, Earls of Oxford, formerly of Hedingham Castle. This is shown to be the more probable by the fact that we have still no less than five examples of the sign in the county, while the adjacent counties of Kent, Middlesex, and Herts possess none. Elsewhere, too, the sign is very uncommon. Not a single example now appears in Surrey, Sussex, Durham, Devonshire, Nottinghamshire, Derbyshire, Northumberland, Cumberland, Westmoreland, or Cheshire. Norfolk, Kent, and Cambridge have one each. Leicestershire and Suffolk (in which county the De Veres also had

BLUE BOAR.

MULLET.

WHISTLE.

WINDLASS.

(*Badges of the De Veres.*)

large estates) have, however, two each. In London, although there is both a BOAR'S HEAD and a BLUE BOAR'S HEAD, there is not now a BLUE BOAR. However, a tradesman's token issued "at the Bleu Boore without Bishopsgate" in the seventeenth century still exists. Much valuable information concerning the *Blue Boar* as used by the De Veres, is contained in a paper by the Rev. H. L. Elliot, of Gosfield, *On Some Badges and Devices of the De Veres, on the Tower of Castle Hedingham Church*.[1] Four of these—the Boar, the Mullet, the Whistle, and the Windlass—are here reproduced.

[1] *Trans. Essex Archæological Soc.*, N. S., vol. ii. part iv. p. 335.

The motto of the family, *Vero nihil verius* and *Verite .vient* formed a rebus on the name. The boar as a badge was evidently assumed for the same reason. The Latin name for the animal is *verres*, though the De Veres probably got it through the Dutch (*veer* or *vere*), as they were a branch of the House of Blois, and owned the Lordship of Vere in Zetland. The boar has been a favourite device of the De Veres from a very early period. The feet of the cross-legged and mail-clad figure of Robert, the fifth Earl, who died in 1296, still existing at Earls Colne Priory, are placed against a boar, and the same animal appears in different capacities on all, or nearly all, the other exist-ing monuments of the family. Stowe speaks of John, the sixteenth Earl, "riding into the city, to his house by London Stone, with eighty gentlemen in a livery of Reading tawney, and chains of gold about their necks, before him, and one hundred tall yeomen in the like livery to follow him, without chains, but all hav-ing his cognizance of the Blew Boar embroydered on

BADGE OF THE DE VERES.
(*From the Black Boy, Chelmsford.*)

their left shoulder." As a badge, the boar is carved, alter-nately with the mullet (another device of the De Veres [1]), over the clerestory windows of Castle Hedingham Church; on several parts of Lavenham Church, Suffolk; on the roof of the south aisle of Sible Hedingham Church; over the west door of Chelmsford Church, and elsewhere. In the Chelms-ford Museum, moreover, is preserved a wooden boss, taken from the ceiling of a room of the old BLACK BOY Inn when it was pulled down. On this is carved a boar, within a circular ribbon charged with seven mullets. Some information as to how these devices came into these positions is given here-

[1] See *post*.

after. For close upon five centuries this mighty family, whose riches were immense, and whose power was second only to that of the sovereign, ruled over a large portion of East Anglia in semi-regal fashion. For 567 years, too, was the same title retained in this one family. It is no wonder, therefore, that their armorial bearings should have been largely used as signs by those who were in various ways dependent upon them ; but it is interesting to find at the present day such comparatively clear evidence of this fact. The principal Essex inn exhibiting the sign of the BLUE BOAR (and the one from which, in all probability, some, at least, of our others have taken the name) was the once famous BLUE BOAR at Castle Hedingham. This ancient house may be cited as a good example of an inn deriving its sign directly

THE WHITE BOAR.
(*Badge of Richard III.*)

from the armorial bearings of a great historical family which formerly resided in the immediate vicinity, and, without doubt, owned the house. Its sign, of course, represented the badge of the mighty Earls of Oxford. The inn was a fine old house standing in St. James's Street, where its ornamental chimneys once formed the most prominent feature. After being injured by fire it was pulled down in 1865. On this occasion various old coins and other relics were discovered, the most interesting being an inscription in Early English characters, written in chalk on a blackened beam behind the wainscot. It ran thus :—

> " Hans pes withe yore nebor whilom ye maye,
> For oftyn tymes favore do the passe withe ye daye."

This may be translated as follows :—

> " Be at peace with your neighbour while ye may,
> For often times the favour will pass with the day."

According to the authors of the *History of Sign-boards* (p. 116), this sign was originally a *white* boar, and represented the *boar argent*, which formed the favourite badge of Richard III., as well as one (or, more generally, both) of the supporters of his arms.

" The fondness of Richard for this badge appears from his wardrobe accounts for the year 1483, one of which contains a charge 'for 8,000 bores made and wrought upon fustian,' and 5,000 more are mentioned shortly afterwards. He also established a herald of arms called ' Blanc Sanglier,' and it was this trusty squire who carried his master's mangled body from Bosworth battle-field to Leicester. . . . After Richard's defeat and death the WHITE BOARS were changed into BLUE BOARS, this being the easiest and cheapest way of changing the sign ; and so the [WHITE] BOAR of Richard, now painted 'true blue,' passed for the [BLUE] BOAR of the Earl of Oxford, who had largely contributed to place Henry VII. on the throne."

Shakespeare in Richard III. (act v., scene 3) alludes to the dead king and his badge as follows:—

> " The wretched, bloody, and usurping boar
> That spoiled your summer fields and fruitful vines ;
> . . . This foul swine . . . lies now . . .
> Near to the town of Leicester, as we learn."

It is related that in this king's reign one William Colling-bourne was executed for composing the following couplet :—

> " The Cat, the Rat, and Lovell our Dog,
> Rule all Englonde under an Hogge."

The king and his ministers, Sir Richard Ratcliffe, Sir William Catesby, and Lord Lovell, were, of course, thus referred to. At Earls Colne, as already stated (p. 63), there is a LION AND BOAR. Here, in all probability, we have again represented the boar of the De Veres, Colne Priory having been another seat of the family, some members of which lie buried there. Other signs, which have, in all probability, been derived (partly, at least) from other badges of the De Veres, will be noticed hereafter.

The sign of the FLITCH OF BACON is most conveniently described in connection with the boar. The authors just quoted say (p. 420), " The FLITCH OF DUNMOW is a common sign in Essex, and is sometimes seen in other counties ; " but it does not appear that we have had more than one in the county for forty years past, that one being, of course, the well-known inn at *Little Dunmow. How the sign originated is too well known to need any explanation here. A similar custom has occasioned a similar sign at Wichnor, near Lichfield (*Gent's Mag.*, 1819). A beer-shop, about thirty years old, in the market-place at Romford, is known by the appropriate name of the PIG IN THE POUND. A PIG AND WHISTLE is in existence at Thames Haven, and there are beer-shops of the same name in Broomfield and Writtle parishes. The origin of this sign appears not to have come down to us out of the mists of antiquity. Very many and very learned are the explanations which have, of late, been proposed as the solution of it. Half the European languages have been ransacked for its derivation, but so far without any satisfactory results. Larwood and Hotten dismiss it as "simply a freak of the mediæval artist." Possibly it may represent, in a corrupted form, the peg said to have been placed in the wassail-bowl by King Edgar, who, in order to discourage drunkenness, imposed a penalty upon any one who drank so deeply as to leave it uncovered. There is, however, a by-no-means-unlikely origin for the sign, and one which the author believes has never before been suggested. In Mr. Elliot's interesting paper just quoted (p. 70) it is stated that, in addition to the *blue boar*, the De Veres, among several other devices, made use of a *Whistle and Chain* as a household badge. Thus, among the devices of this one family, are found the two objects—a pig (or boar) and a whistle—which, when combined, constitute this most perplexing sign. It is very difficult — perhaps impossible—to prove now that the sign was actually derived from these two badges of the De Veres, but, remembering the enormous past importance of the family, it must be admitted that the sign was in no way unlikely to have been so derived. Mr. Elliot himself writes that he considers this suggestion not unlikely to be the correct one. Very probably this description of the Earl's badges was a derisive one, applied to them by the Yorkist party during the Wars of the Roses. A whistle, like that adopted by the De Veres, was formerly worn by sea-captains, even of high rank; and Mr. Elliot is of opinion that it was assumed by the De Veres as a symbol of the office of Lord High Admiral, an appointment held by John, the thirteenth Earl, who was very active on behalf of the Lancastrian party.

Forty-six inns in Essex exhibit signs which are more or less canine. A few of these may have had their origin in Heraldry; but there can be no doubt that, in the great majority of cases, the signs have originated in the modern use of the dog, whether for sporting or other purposes. At Wethersfield and Halstead the Dog appears alone; at East Horndon there is an Old Dog; a Pointer exists at Alresford; and at Colchester, East Mersey, and Tolleshunt Knights the Dog and Pheasant appears; while at Stifford and Great Leighs (beer-house) the Dog and Partridge is used, as it was also at *Halstead sixty years ago. The sign of the Spotted Dog, although it is not mentioned by Hotten, occurs four times, namely at Witham, Barking, Chelmsford, and West Ham, and there is a beer-house of the same name at Braintree. The sole use of the Spotted, or Dalmatian, Dog in this country, says a writer in the *Gentleman's Magazine*, "is to contribute, by the beauty of its appearance, to the splendour of the stable establishment, constantly attending the horses and carriage to which he belongs." On October 22, 1804, a disastrous and fatal fire took place at the Spotted Dog, *Chelmsford. The details are given in a scarce pamphlet, reprinted in Hughson's *London* (vol. vi. p. 246). It seems that about 120 Hanoverian soldiers marched into Chelmsford on the day in question, and about 70 of them took up their lodgings in the stables of this inn. While most of them were asleep it was discovered that the straw upon which they lay had caught fire. All were, of course, at once aroused, but being unused to the fastening of the door, they were unable to open it. When at last it was opened and the inmates liberated, many of them were sorely burned, and others had their clothing on fire. The flames were got under after a time, but not until they had extended to other stables and burned several horses. On clearing away the rubbish, the bodies of no less than thirteen of the Hanoverian soldiers who had perished in the flames were found. They were afterwards buried with military honours in the church. At Hordon-on-the-Hill there is a Black Dog (beer-house). The Shepherd and Dog is a device which is now to be seen at Upminster, Ramsden Cray, and Great Stambridge (beer-house). Two centuries ago it appeared on the farthing token of " Peeter Pearcce " of Braintree ; while a DOG WITH CHAIN, *passant*, occurs on that of "Thomas Peeke, Wyre Street, in Colchstr," and a dog eating out of a flesh-pot (the DOG'S HEAD IN POT) on the halfpenny issued by John Phillips of Plaistow in 1670. This device seems to have been originally used to indicate a dirty, slovenly housewife. It was never common. The HARE AND HOUNDS occurs seven times, the FOX AND HOUNDS ten times, and the HUNTSMAN AND HOUNDS once (at Upminster). Both the FOX and the FOX AND HOUNDS are very common beer-house signs. The HARE, an unusual sign when not accompanied by the Hounds, appears at Great Parndon. The TALBOT at North Weald may be named after the famous TALBOT in Southwark, which, under its former name of the TABARD, sheltered Chaucer's pilgrims on their way to Canterbury. Talbot is the name of an old variety of hunting dog which, at the present day, is never heard of except in connection with Heraldry; and, as the sign in question is not now a pictorial one, most of the inhabitants of North Weald would probably be much puzzled to explain what it originally represented. There was another TALBOT in Stapleford Tawney until about ten years ago, but it is now a private house. The county contains no less than thirteen GREYHOUNDS, one of which is an OLD GREYHOUND. The sign of the GREYHOUND existed at Chelmsford in 1786, according to the *Chelmsford Chronicle* for July 21st in that year, but it is not now extant, though Greyhound Lane still exists. In all probability this was the house that existed under the same name in 1662, as mentioned in the *Account of the Murder of Thomas Kidderminster*, to which reference has been already made. The GREYHOUND at Waltham Abbey is mentioned in the parish

DOG'S HEAD IN POT.
(After Larwood and Hotten.)

registers on June 4, 1735, when " John Munns from yᵉ Greyhound was Bur." The GREYHOUND at Barking is mentioned in the parish register as early as 1592.[1] An entry states that " Henry, the supposed son of Henry Fisher of London, from the Greyhound, was bapᵈ the 17th of October." For this sign we are probably about equally indebted both to the sport of coursing and the art of Heraldry. *Greyhounds argent* formed either one or both of the supporters of Henry VII., the badge, and often one of the supporters, of Henry VIII., and one of the supporters of Elizabeth and Mary ; so that in all probability the sign found its origin in Heraldry, but owes its use in the present day, largely at least, to coursing.

In a hunting district like Essex it is in no way surprising that there should be as many as twenty-five references to the fox on our sign-boards. Although twenty years ago the sign of the Fox only occurred five times, it now occurs eleven times ; while there are ten signs of the Fox AND HOUNDS, and three of the Fox AND GOOSE. The latter is a combination which mediæval artists never tired of representing. It may be seen, among other places, on a carved oak screen in Hadstock Church. Of the FLYING Fox at Colchester, Larwood and Hotten say (p. 170) — " It may represent some kind of bat or flying squirrel (?) so denominated, or is a landlord's caprice." It seems much more probable, however, that the device is intended to represent a fox flying before the hounds.

There is a beer-house known as the WOLF at Great Coggeshall. The origin of the sign, which is not mentioned by Larwood and Hotten, is hard to explain. Probably it is unique.

The sign of the HARE AND HOUNDS, of which, as previously stated (p. 76), we have seven examples, is, doubtless, entirely derived from the sport of coursing ; but the RABBITS, a very old house still in existence at Little Ilford, has probably an heraldic origin. Most likely the sign is derived from three coneys appearing on some family coat of arms, but

[1] *Trans. Essex Arch. Soc.*, vol. ii. p. 128.

whose, it is now difficult to say. The sign appeared in the
list as the THREE RABBITS forty years ago, and as the THREE
CONEYS on Jean Roque's *Map of Ten Miles Round London*,
published in 1746. Lysons, in his *Environs of London* (1796,
vol. iv. p. 157), says—

> "A great mart for cattle from Wales, Scotland, and the North of
> England is held annually, from the latter end of February till the begin-
> ning of May, on the flat part of the forest of Waltham (commonly called
> Epping Forest), within the parishes of Ilford, Eastham, Westham, Ley-
> ton, and Wanstead. A great part of the business between the dealers
> is transacted at the RABBITS in this parish—on the high road."

There is also a beer-shop known as the RABBITS in Stapleford Tawney parish. It is probably named after the foregoing. There is another beer-house so called at West
Thurrock. Larwood and Hotten do not mention the sign
under any of the above forms, although they say that in
1667 Hugh Conny, of Caxton and Elsworth, Cambridge, had
THREE CONIES for a sign, and a RABBIT is depicted on the
farthing token of one William Hutchenson, of Chelmsford.

The sign of the FLEECE occurs twice at *Colchester, once
at *Coggeshall, and once at Brentwood. That of the

FLEECE.

GOLDEN FLEECE appears at Chelmsford
and East Ham, although the former seems
to have become golden only during the last
forty years. There were also FLEECES at
Halstead and Witham sixty years ago.
Both forms of the sign are, of course, intended to represent Jason's Golden Fleece,
or Gideon's, and their use commemorates
the time when the woollen trade was one
of the staple industries of Essex. The Fleece also formed
the pendant of the Order of the GOLDEN FLEECE, which
was founded in 1429 by Philip, Duke of Burgundy and
Count of Flanders, "to perpetuate the memory of his
great revenues raised by wools with the Low Countries,"
as Ashmole says. Ancient encaustic tiles have been
found, Mr. Elliot writes, both in Witham and Maldon
(St. Mary's) Churches bearing the arms of the Dukes of

Burgundy, with their badge of flint, steel, and sparks in the upper and side spandrels, and the figure of the Fleece below. A fleece forms a charge in the arms of the town of Leeds,[1] now the principal seat of the woollen trade. Larwood and Hotten facetiously remark that "a fleece at the door of an inn or public-house looks very like a warning of the fate a traveller may expect within." The STAR AND FLEECE is an odd combination, which does not appear to be noticed in the *History of Sign-boards*. It may simply be an impaled sign, or may represent the fleece of one of the mullets in the arms of Leeds. An example has existed at Kelvedon for over forty years, and another was in existence a few years since. Another emblem of the woollen trade is the WOOLPACK, of which, as already stated (p. 39), we have six examples, arranged in an almost straight line across the county, namely, at *Romford, Ingatestone, Chelmsford, Witham, *Coggeshall, and *Colchester. Three, at least, of these were in existence sixty years since, at which time there was another at Bocking. It is recorded in *Bufton's Diary*[2] that on May 1, 1693, at Coggeshall, "Yᶜ soldiers set up a Maypole at yᶜ WOOLPACKE doore." The WOOLPACK is a device which appears commonly on the tokens of the seventeenth century. It is met with at Billericay, Dunmow, Castle Hedingham (twice), Braintree, Bocking, Witham, and Colchester. The sign of the WOOLPACK, it should be noticed, is still, or was lately, to be seen at the three last-named places. The sign of the SHEARS, as pointed out elsewhere (p. 41), is another relic of the now departed woollen trade. From the middle of the seventeenth to the end of the eighteenth century, the spinning, carding, and weaving of wool formed the staple industry in most of the larger towns and villages of Eastern England. Several prominent families of the district in former days owed their wealth to this trade. In the neighbourhood of Hedingham it is said that several old houses, of which remnants only

---

[1] Azure ; a fleece or; on a chief of the last, three mullets of five points of the first.

[2] Dale's *Annals of Coggeshall*, p. 267.

now exist, were once "wool-halls," combining a residence
for the merchant with a warehouse for his wools, worsteds,
and "pieces." Very high wages were earned by the work-
people, even by children and old persons. It has been estimated that, at the middle of last century, not less than
20,000 hands in and around Colchester were employed in
the woollen trade; but by the end of the century the number
had sunk to less than 8,000. Many old persons still living
can remember their parents' or grand-parents' accounts of
the festivities on St. Blaize's Day, the 3rd of February, when
there were processions in mediæval fashion, with shepherdess
and lamb, and men and women spinning and weaving, accompanied by a great deal of noise and fun, bell-ringing
and band - playing, ribbons and banners, roystering and
drinking. In the evening bonfires were lit upon the hills to
commemorate (as the common people thought) the name
of their patron, St. Blaize. The weaving of bunting for
ships' flags lingered in and around Sudbury until about
twenty years ago, but has now quite died out in East Anglia.
The RAM, at North Woolwich, perhaps, represents the crest
of the Clothworkers' Company.[1] Our six examples of the
sign of the LAMB may, or may not, have had an heraldic
origin. They probably represent the Lamb with the flag of
the Apocalypse; but this was used as a crest by the Merchant
Taylors' Company.[2] The farthing issued in 1654 by "Tho.
Lambe at Bvttls Gate in Colchester" bears a *Holy Lamb
couchant*, and that of "Joseph Lamb of Lee [Leigh], 1664,"
bears the same device. In both cases a rebus or pun on the
name of the issuer is, of course, intended. The LAMBS at *Colchester and *Romford are both at least sixty years old. Probably the sign was first set up as an emblem of the woollen trade.
The five instances in which the Lamb occurs in conjunction
with a Lion have already been noticed (p. 63), and attention
has also been drawn to the fact (p. 23) that some, at least, of

---

[1] A mount vert, thereon a ram statant.

[2] Argent; a royal tent between two parliament robes gules, lined
ermine; on a chief azure, a lion passant guardant or. *Crest:* On a
mount vert, a lamb passant argent, holding a banner of the last, staff
proper, on the banner a cross pattée gules within a glory of the third.

our SHIPS are probably intended for *sheep*. The SHOULDER
OF MUTTON, which occurs both at Great Totham and Ford-
ham, probably represents the joint so often brought to table.

The BEAR occurs by himself only twice, namely, at Buttsbury (where he is at least forty years old), and at Romford.
The BEAR at Buttsbury is mentioned in the Stock parish
registers in 1673. Forty years ago there were also BEARS at
Colchester and Great Baddow. We are probably more indebted
to the old custom of bear-baiting for this sign than to Heraldry.
Larwood and Hotten say that it was originally adopted by alehouses as a pun on the word " beer." If so, the pun was a
very weak one. The WHITE BEAR is to be seen at Galleywood and at Stanford Rivers. At the latter place he has
existed at least since 1789, and is represented on a board over
the door, but not upon the swinging sign-board, as a Polar
Bear picking his way over blocks of ice. The sign of the
WHITE BEAR is not a modern one. It was used in the
seventeenth century, and both of our Essex examples are
over forty years old. The Queen of Richard III. used a
White Bear as her badge, and this perhaps originated the
sign.

Of the ELEPHANT AND CASTLE, a very old device, we have
two instances in Essex, one at Harwich, and the other at
Colchester. Neither seems to have been in existence twenty
years ago. Most probably they are named after the famous
old coaching inn at Newington Butts ; but they may have
originally been cutlers' signs. The elephant with a castle
on his back (as he was generally represented in the Middle
Ages) formed the crest of the Cutlers' Company.[1] At Great
Baddow, Rayleigh, and elsewhere the device serves as a
beer-house sign.

The GOAT AND BOOTS on *East Hill, Colchester, though
over forty years old, is a sign which is not noticed in the
History of Sign-boards. It is, doubtless, a corruption of the
not-uncommon sign of the GOAT IN BOOTS, which appears
to be a caricature of Welshmen, and not a corruption of the

[1] An elephant argent, armed or, on his back a tower of the first, the
trappings, &c., of the second.

7

Dutch description of Mercury, *der goden boode* (the gods' messenger), as is often stated. We have in Essex no example of the not-uncommon sign of the GOAT AND COMPASSES, which is usually supposed to be a corruption of the Puritan motto, " God encompasses us." This explanation, however, is not sound. The motto could never have been represented pictorially upon the sign-board, and we know that pictorial representation was the sole aim and object of the sign in olden times. Probably the sign is merely a compound one; or it may represent the arms of the Cordwainers' Company [1] in a corrupted form. To this origin may be certainly traced the sign of the THREE GOATS' HEADS, which, however, does not occur in Essex.

The SQUIRREL'S HEAD at Squirrel's Heath, Romford, has no doubt some connection with the locality. It was not in existence forty years ago. The sign of the THREE SQUIRRELS, which is not found in Essex, has been in use for over two centuries.

The sign of the SEA HORSE, which has existed at *Colchester for at least sixty years past, is not noticed by Larwood and Hotten. Very likely it commemorates the capture in the Colne, and subsequent exhibition in the town, of some such strange creature as a seal or porpoise, which vulgar belief set down as a " sea horse."

The sign of the DOLPHIN occurs four times in the county, namely, at *Colchester, *Chelmsford, Maldon, and *Romford. The animal also figures as a beer-house sign at Stisted, Goldhanger, &c. The houses bearing it may have taken their sign from the many representations of the dolphin in private coats of arms; but, most likely, they have simply been called after the famous DOLPHIN Inn which existed in London for several centuries, and is said to have been occupied by Louis, the Dauphin of France, who, in 1216, came over to contest the English crown with King John. It was once adorned with fleurs-de-lys, dolphins, and other French cognizances. The dolphin formed the badge of the Dauphins of France, just as the three ostrich feathers form the badge

---

[1] Azure ; a chevron or, between three goats' heads erased argent.

of our own Princes of Wales. Larwood and Hotten do not notice the sign of the WHALEBONE of which Essex possesses four examples, namely, at Woodham Ferrers, *Colchester, Fingringhoe, and White Roothing. That at the latter place has apparently been in existence for at least a century, as it is mentioned more than once in the *Chelmsford Chronicle* in the year 1786, while the one at Colchester figured in the list as the OLD WHALEBONE forty years ago. The FISH-BONE, however, spoken of by Larwood and Hotten as being " rarely met with as a public-house sign," though frequently used by dealers in rags and bones, is probably the same sign under a different name. In the museum at Saffron Walden there has been, for nearly fifty years past, a large whale's scapula, which is said formerly to have hung as a sign in one of the streets of that town. Mr. Joseph Clarke believes it was displayed at the KING'S HEAD, and it has on it an almost illegible letter R, probably part of the monogram G. R.; but more likely it formed the sign of the WHALE-BONE at some house not now in existence, or not under that name. Of the SUN AND WHALEBONE which has existed at Latton since 1789 at least, the authors so frequently quoted say that " it may have originated from a whalebone hanging outside the house or [it may indicate] that the landlord had laid the foundation of his fortune as a rag merchant." More probably, however, its origin was the impalement of two distinct signs. The sign-board is not pictorial. This sign was very fully discussed in *Notes and Queries* in 1862 (3rd series, vol. i. pp. 250, 335, 359, 397, 419, and 473). Several most profound speculations were advanced to account for it, but they were all more or less far fetched. The WHALE-BONE at Chadwell Heath has now disappeared, though a beer-shop so named existed there until about the year 1870. From it, in all probability, our four existing houses of this name, as well as the SUN AND WHALEBONE at Latton, have taken their designation; for the sign is a very uncommon one in the adjoining counties, and does not appear at all in London. The house in question originally took its name from two whale's jaw-bones (not *rib*-bones, as is commonly supposed) set up in the form of an archway over the road close at hand. Local tradition says that the bones were those of a whale that was stranded in the Thames near Dagenham during the great storm that prevailed on the night preceding September 3, 1658, when Oliver Cromwell died.

This was, perhaps, the case, as "Ye Whalebone" is marked against the tenth milestone from London on the map of the high-road from London to Harwich, given in Ogilby's *Itinerarium Angliæ*, published in 1675, only seventeen years after the whale is said to have been stranded. Also in Dr. Howell's *Ancient and Present State of England*, first published in 1678, it is stated (6th Ed. p. 263) that, "near about this time [1658], there came up the Thames as far as Greenwich a whale of very great length and bigness." Daniel Defoe, too, in his *Tour through the whole Island of Great Britain*, first published in 1724, says (vol. i. p. 3) the WHALE-BONE was "so called because the rib-bone of a large Whale, taken in the River of Thames, was fixed there in 1658, the year Oliver Cromwell died, for a monument of that monstrous creature, it being at first about Eight and Twenty Foot long." The WHALE'S BONE is also marked on *Andrew and Drury's Map of Essex*, published in 1777. That a storm of most unusual magnitude did rage on the night in question, is certain. Prideaux, in his *Introduction to History* (1682), speaks of "that most horrid tempestuous night which ushered in this day [on which Cromwell died]." Pepys also mentions the storm. Nor is it anything new for whales and similar animals to appear in the Thames. In Sir Richard Baker's *Chronicles of the Kings of England* (p. 425), published in 1684, it is recorded that on the 19th of January, 1606, "a great Porpus was taken at West Ham, in a small creek a mile and a half within the land ; and within a few days after a Whale came up within eight miles of London, whose body was seen divers times above the water, and was judged to exceed the length of the largest ship in the River: but when she tasted the fresh water and scented the land, she returned again into the sea." On the morning of April 31, 1879, too, a whale alarmed some fishermen by his spouting near Hole Haven. Many other records might be cited. It is, however, a curious circumstance that in M. J. Farmer's *History of Waltham Abbey*, published in 1735, there is given as an appendix " The Inquisition taken the 17th of King Charles I. [1642] of a Perambulation of Waltham Forest in the County of Essex," in which occurs the following passage :—[The Forest boundary runs] "from Great Ilford directly by the same King's High Way leading towards Rumford, to a certain *Quadrivium* (or way leading four ways), called the Four Wants, where late was placed and yet is a certain side of a whale, called the *Whale bone.*" From this it would appear that the spot was known as the Whalebone long before Cromwell's death. Possibly, however, there is an error in the above date, Charles I. being inserted instead of Charles II.

A good deal of discussion upon the subject took place several years ago in the pages of *Notes and Queries.* In 1871 (p. 4), "G. S." wrote that he had often seen whales' bones set upright in Holland for cattle to rub against, and that he "was once struck with the same in a large park between Ingatestone and Chelmsford. The owner was a Dutch gentleman, who had introduced this sensible idea into England." Other correspondents wrote that they knew of whales' bones having been set up in various parts of England. Later on (p. 195), Mr. J. Perry, of Waltham Abbey, wrote that—

" There is (or was lately) a pair of whale's ribs placed over the old toll-gate at Chadwell Heath, near Romford, Essex, which form a kind of Gothic arch across the roadway. They must have been there for a considerable period, as it is beyond the memory of any of the good old country-folks living in the locality to tell when first erected. At a little distance from the toll-house occurs a similar pair, set up over the carriage entrance to a residence."

Afterwards (1878, p. 397) " S. P." wrote as follows :—

"When I was a boy, there stood by the roadside, about two miles west of Romford, at the east end of the long straggling village of Chadwell Heath, and on the left hand going from London, a tremendous pair of bones, forming an arch. The bases were deeply rooted in the earth, but even then the space spanned was considerable. Near by was a toll-house, with its bar, known from the adjacent relic as ' Whalebone Gate.' I think, too, if I remember rightly, there stood near the spot a road-side inn called by the sign of 'the WHALEBONE.' My father, an Essex man, long since dead, used to tell me that he had it from his grandfather, that the bone was the upper [should be lower] jaw of an immense whale, which had been cast ashore about three miles to the south of the spot, on the north bank of the Thames, at Dagenham, while the Great Storm was raging on the night that Oliver Cromwell died. In course of time, toll on suburban roads was abolished ; the toll-house and gate were cleared away ; and the jaw was appropriated to serve as an entrance arch to the front garden of a neighbouring suburban villa—the rural residence, I believe, of a Whitechapel pork-butcher—an edifice known, and still indicated on suburban maps of a tolerably modern date, as ' Whalebone House.' . . . What became of the worthy tradesman I have above alluded to, I do not know. Probably his house is still standing, but I am unable to identify it now by its former title or peculiar gate. I am under the impression that what remains of the relic has been transferred to its original site ; for I was past the spot where, so far as my memory serves me, it formerly stood, on July 25th in this year. Half the arch (*i.e.*, one bone) stood upright, still deeply rooted in the earth, but alone, forgotten and deserted, by the side of the high road in a fallow field. No one in the neighbourhood seemed to know anything about it or its history."

To this, Mr. J. A. Sparvel-Bayly, of Billericay, wrote (1879, p. 58) :—

" In the little village of East Tilbury in Essex, situate on the banks of the Thames, and not far from Romford, is a house known as 'Whalebone Cottage,' in front of which is an arch composed of the jawbones of a huge whale. From their weather-worn appearance they may possibly have belonged to that alluded to by S. P."

In reply to this, Mr. W. Phillips (p. 338) stated that—

" The jawbones spoken of by Mr. Sparvel-Bayly as being at East Tilbury, ' not far from Romford' (it is twelve miles from Romford as the crow flies), cannot be identical with those mentioned by S. P., whose account I can corroborate, so far as knowing the jawbones he mentions, forty years ago, when travelling on the box-seat of the old Colchester Coach alongside a coachman of the Mr. Weller sort, of some sixty-five summers. The two bones were then in existence on the north side of the road near the tenth milestone, and two miles the London side of Romford, in front of a roadside public-house with the sign of the 'WHALEBONE,' which my coachman said used to be the resort of the many highwaymen that once infested Chadwell Heath close by. He spoke of his being told when a boy that the bones had been there from the time of Cromwell."

From the foregoing, it is clear that there were formerly *two* pairs of bones set up near together; indeed, Mr. J. Perry distinctly says there were. One pair has now entirely disappeared. The other pair still stand (although S. P. seems to have overlooked them), as described, over the entrance of an adjoining house, known to this day as " Whalebone

House" or "Lodge," and marked as such in local directories. There is also in the immediate vicinity a " Whalebone Farm," as well as a " Whalebone Lane." The bones (of which an illustration is here given) are of the following dimensions :—

	Feet.	Inches.
Height out of ground (along curve)	15	6
Circumference (at base)	3	3½
„ (near top).................................	2	0
Breadth at base (flat inner side)......................	1	5
„ (round outer side)	1	10½

GATEWAY AT WHALEBONE HOUSE.
(*Chadwell Heath.*)

If, as seems probable, the bones are those of the Greenland whale (*Balœna mysticetus*), it is extremely unlikely that the creature which owned them was ever stranded in the Thames. The following letter from Prof. W. H. Flower, F.R.S., is of much interest. He says—

" Pairs of the lower jawbones of the Greenland whale, erected usually as gate-posts, occur in many parts of the eastern counties, especially in the neighbourhood of the old whaling-ports—the Thames, Yarmouth, Hull, Whitby, &c. They have all been brought from the Arctic Seas by whalers, at any time since 1611, when the first ships left England for the Spitzbergen whaling, which (with the Baffin's Bay whaling) has been carried on with more or less success ever since, though now confined to Peterhead and Dundee. I very much doubt Defoe's '28 feet long.' Twenty feet, following the curve, is the maximum of the Greenland whale, and no other whale has such large jaws. I also doubt the story of the creature being stranded, because, if so, it cannot have been a Greenland whale—a species which never visits our shores."

Larwood and Hotten, in common with nearly all heraldic writers, innocently treat of whales and dolphins as *fishes*, as they were commonly supposed to be in the Middle Ages. A writer in *All the Year Round*, so lately as the year 1879, commits the same absurd error.

It will here be necessary to ask pardon of modern men of science for discussing, under the heading "Zoology," certain monstrous beasts which, though unknown to us in these enlightened times, were accredited with a material existence by the ancient heralds, and others who wrote in the dark days of several centuries ago. Such imaginary creatures as dragons, griffins, unicorns, and the like, are, of [course, here referred to.

The DRAGON in his own proper colour (whatever that may be) does not occur in the county; but we have four examples of the GREEN DRAGON, situated respectively at Shenfield, Black Notley, *Saffron Walden, and Waltham Abbey. Sixty years ago there were also GREEN DRAGONS at *Colchester and elsewhere. It is very easy to account for the origin of the use of the Dragon as a sign, but it is not so easy to say why he should so often be green. The

DRAGON.

GREEN DRAGON, however, has been a common sign for over two centuries. As the badge and supporter of the arms of many of our sovereigns, he was generally red, though occasionally black or golden. The Dragon appeared on the standard of the Saxons, and was used as a badge by several early Princes of Wales. It formed one or other of the supporters of the arms of Henry VII., and of all the Tudor sovereigns except Queen Mary. It appears also in the heraldic bearings of many private families. There can, therefore, be very little doubt as to its heraldic derivation, although it was formerly used as a chemist's sign, in which case its origin was probably non-heraldic. Perhaps, as the Rev. H. L. Elliot writes, the strange colour in which this monster usually appears on sign-boards is due to the fact that a Green Dragon, holding in his mouth a bloody hand, was a badge of William Herbert, Lord Steward, created Earl of Pembroke in the time of Edward VI. The GEORGE AND DRAGON is a sign which occurs eight times in Essex.

This very common sign has increased greatly in popularity since the institution of the Order of the Garter, of which a representation of St. George killing a dragon forms the pendant; but the fact that several of our recent kings have borne the name of George has no doubt had a good deal to do with its adoption. The legendary act of St. George, the patron-saint of England, is alluded to in the following amusing little rhyme:—

> " To save a mayd, St. George the Dragon slew—
> A pretty tale, if all that's told be true.
> Most say there are no dragons, and 'tis sayd
> There was no George ;—let's hope there was a mayd."

A representation of St. George killing the Dragon appears on the token issued by J. Lark of Coggeshall in 1667.[1]

There are also in Essex three examples of the sign of the GRIFFIN, situated respectively at Great Canfield, Halstead, and Danbury. The GRIFFIN at Danbury, an ancient and well-known inn, is mentioned in the *Chelmsford Chronicle* on May 9, 1788. It is also several times prominently alluded to (ii. p. 174, iii. pp. 130 and 144, and iv. p. 66) in Mr. Joseph Strutt's Essex and Herts Romance of *Queenhoo Hall*, published in 1808. Although in former ages people firmly believed in the existence of griffins, the animal has never yet been seen except in Heraldry. Consequently it is only natural to assign the origin of its use as a sign to that art; but griffins appear upon the escutcheons of so many families that it is now quite impossible to say in whose honour it made its first appearance upon the sign-board.

GRIFFIN.

The UNICORN appears as a public-house sign at West Ham and at Romford. At the latter place the house is situated in Hare Street, and is at least a century old, as it is mentioned in the *Chelmsford Chronicle* for March 2, 1787. A

---

[1] It is worth mention here that in the *Account of the Trials of John Swan and Elizabeth Jeffries*, published in 1752, reference is made (p. 10) to a certain " John Mills [who resided] at the WHY NOT BEAT DRAGON? at Mile End." This most extraordinary sign, however, is just outside Essex. Larwood and Hotten do not allude to it.

unicorn rampant is depicted on the farthing tokens of William Alldred of Colchester, and a *unicorn passant* on those of " Will. Anger of Mvch Clafton [? Clacton] in Esex, 1654." The original use of the UNICORN as an inn-sign may be attributed to the fact that it was formerly a common chemist's sign, and is one of the supporters of the arms of the Apothecaries' Company, or to the fact that it now forms the sinister supporter of the Royal Arms. Much interesting information as to the ancient belief in its existence, and the power of its horn as an antidote to all poison, is given in the *History of Sign-boards*.

CHAPTER IV.

ORNITHOLOGICAL SIGNS.

RNITHOLOGICAL signs stand next in turn for notice. They are fairly numerous, and many are of strictly heraldic derivation. The Eagle appears in one form or another on nineteen Essex sign-boards. On seven occasions a simple EAGLE is intended. Twenty years ago, however, there were but three. Ten times the sign of the SPREAD EAGLE occurs, and the same device is depicted on the tokens issued by John Millbank of Colchester in 1665, and by Samuel Wall of Witham in 1668. The SPREAD EAGLE at Harwich, which is a house still extant, is referred to in the issue of the *Chelmsford Chronicle* for March 31, 1786. At Little Bardfield a carved and gilded SPREAD EAGLE is set up on the top of a post before the inn. The sign is truly heraldic, inasmuch as the bird does not seem to require to use its legs, but stands upon its tail. In the *Chelmsford Chronicle* for March 2, 1787, there appears an advertisement stating that a " Main of Cocks " was to be fought on the 7th of that month at the *SPREAD EAGLE in

SPREAD EAGLE.

Prittlewell, between the Gentlemen of that place and the Gentlemen of Great Wakering. Eagles occur so frequently in Heraldry that there can be no doubt whence the sign of the EAGLE is derived; and the fact that the bird is, more often than not, described as " spread," goes far to confirm its heraldic derivation. An eagle was displayed upon the ensign of the Roman emperors, and has since formed one of the chief

cognizances of the sovereigns of Germany, Russia, Prussia,
Austria, France, &c.   Edward III. bore a crowned eagle as
his crest, and Henry IV. adopted a spread eagle as one of his
badges.   The bird is also of very frequent occurrence in the
armorial bearings of private families.   The EAGLE at Snares-
brook is a well-known old hostelry, and is a very favourite
Bank Holiday resort of " 'Arry and 'Arriet " from the East

End of London.   The EAGLE AND
CHILD, which is to be seen at Shenfield and Forest Gate, is not uncommon elsewhere, and will be at
once recognized as the crest of the
Stanleys, Earls of Derby, which
represents an eagle carrying off a
child, as told in the well-known
legend,[1] and as here depicted.   In a
curious collection of miscellanea
relating to signs formed by a Mr.
G. Creed, and now preserved in the
British Museum, it is stated that in the parlour of the last-
named inn there is (or was in 1850) framed " a MS. bit of
Doggrell," commencing as follows :—

EAGLE AND CHILD.

The Essex Flats too Knowing for the Yorkshire Sharps.

"An Essex Landlord of some fame,
Whose honesty deserves a name,
Near to the Forest hangs his sign,
A house well known for Bowls of wine.
It represents a lovely boy,
Such as would give a father joy ;
Beside him (don't say 'tis absurd)
Stands the majestic kingly Bird,
And both are named and known together,
As birds are known that's of one feather."

The rest of the poem, which is long, does not merit re-
production.   This house is marked on Jean Roque's *Map
of Ten Miles round London*, published in 1741.   The FALCON
occurs three times, namely, at Southend, Littlebury, and

---

[1] On a chapeau gules, turned up ermine, an eagle, wings extended or,
preying on an infant in its cradle proper, swaddled gules, the cradle laced
gules.

Wivenhoe. Twenty years ago one of these figured in the list as the NEW FALCON, and sixty years since there was another in the High Street at *Braintree. A farthing token showing a bird holding a sceptre, and issued by "John Parker at the Falken in Wivenhoe," is described by Boyne. Taylor (see p. 28) also mentions this Parker in 1636. As the sign of the FALCON still exists at Wivenhoe it is probably the same house kept more than two centuries ago by John Parker, especially as the same house is mentioned again in an advertisement in the *Chelmsford Chronicle* for January 13, 1786. At the end of last century there was an inn with the sign of the FALCON close against the Cross at Waltham. Two illustrations of it, published respectively in 1787 and

FALCON.
(*At Waltham Cross in* 1787.)

1791, are preserved in Mr. Creed's collection. They show the sign-board (a pictorial one, inscribed with the name of the landlord—Sibley) suspended from a beam which extends across the road. Above this beam is hung a bunch of grapes within an iron frame, as here shown. The sign has now been altered to that of the GREAT EASTERN.

The OLD FALCON Inn, which formerly existed at Castle Hedingham, though now reduced to a mere beer-shop, was once evidently a very good house. Its beams and rafters are very massive, and bear the crest and badge of the Earls of Oxford, like not a few other old houses in the vicinity. The sign is probably identical with that of the HAWK, which occurs at Battles Bridge. Its origin may have been the ancient sport of hawking; but, more probably, it has an heraldic derivation. A *falcon volant* forms part of the arms of the Stationers' Company, and it was probably adopted by booksellers on this account. Both Edward III. and Richard II. used a falcon as one of their badges, and the FALCON HOLDING A SCEPTRE, which, as just mentioned, existed at Wivenhoe in the seventeenth century, was presumably derived from one of the badges of Queen Elizabeth, *a falcon crowned, holding a sceptre*. It is, however, by no means improbable that the particular instance of the sign of the FALCON in Falcon Square, Castle Hedingham (which happens to be *triangular !*), may be a relic of the ancient family of the Hawkwoods, who resided in the adjoining parish of Sible Hedingham. Sir John Hawkwood, the famous soldier who became so prominent in the Italian wars of the fourteenth century, was buried in Florence, but upon the beautiful crocketted canopy of the monument erected to him in the south aisle of Sible Hedingham Church, his badge (?), a Hawk or Falcon, is carved several times, with other devices.

The Swan, including several variations in colour, &c., is a very common Essex sign, and appears in thirty-eight

WHITE SWAN.
(*The Badge of the De Bohuns.*)

different places; while, forty or fifty years ago, it seems to have been even commoner. Thirty-two times he occurs as a simple SWAN; at Harwich he appears as a NEW SWAN; at Rayne and Roydon (where he is at least one hundred years old) as a BLACK SWAN; at Chelmsford as an OLD SWAN; and at Epping and West Ham as a WHITE SWAN. The SWAN now existing at Brentwood is, apparently, at least a century old, as it is mentioned in the *Chelmsford Chronicle* on March 24, 1786. The fondness of the bird for liquid (though of a purer kind than that usually supplied at public-houses) is said to have been the reason for its very common adoption as a public-house sign ; but the custom is equally likely to have had an heraldic origin. Kings Henry IV. and V. both used a swan among other badges, and the same device formed part of the coat of arms of the De Bohun and other families. The annexed wood-cut of the *swan proper, ducally gorged and chained or,* which formed the badge of the De Bohuns, is taken from the central spandrel of the canopy of the brass in Westminster Abbey to Alianore De Bohun, Duchess of Gloucester, who died in 1399. It is also very probable that the white swan which formed the badge of the great De Mandevilles, once Earls of Essex, has had something to do with the abundance of this sign in the county. In *Tavern Anecdotes* (p. 241) it is stated that in 1825 the landlord of the *Swan at Stratford recommended the charms of his house in the following poetic strain :—

> " At the Swan Tavern kept by Lound
> The best accommodation's found,—
> Wine, Spirits, Porter, Bottled Beer,
> You'll find in high perfection here.
> If in the garden with your lass
> You feel inclined to take a glass,
> There Tea and Coffee of the best
> Provided is, for every guest.
> And, females not to drive from hence,
> The charge is only fifteen pence.
> Or, if disposed a Pipe to smoke,
> To sing a song or crack a joke,
> You may repair across the Green,
> Where nought is heard, though much is seen ;
> There laugh and drink, and smoke away,
> And but a moderate reckoning pay,
> Which is a most important object
> To every loyal British subject.
> In short, the best accommodation's found
> By those who deign to visit Lound."

In Mr. Chas. Golding's *List of Essex Tokens,*[1] pieces inscribed "Abel Bond at ye WHITE [SWAN] in Stratford, His Halfe Penny," and " John Chandler [a SWAN] in Stratford, J. C." are mentioned. The still-existing SWAN at Baythorn End, Birdbrook, appears to be over two centuries

---

[1] Lowestoft, 1867.

old. In the parish register is the following entry : " Martha Blewitt, ye wife of nine husbands successively, buried eight of y^m, but last of all ye woman dy'd allsoe, was bury'd May 7th, 1681." A slab in the Church shows that Martha Blewitt was landlady of the above inn.

In Cromwell's *Excursions through Essex* (i. p. 17) it is stated that " The SWAN, a very large and famous inn, anciently stood in the road near the farm ' called Shakestones." The view of Romford given in Wright's *History of Essex* (1831, ii. p. 435) shows the graven sign of the WHITE SWAN Inn, projecting from the front of the building exactly as it does now. It appears from an old Manor Roll [1] that in 1572 there was a " tenement called the SWAN "—not necessarily an inn—in Coggeshall. The sign still exists there —namely, in East Street—though possibly not at the same house. It is, however, again mentioned in 1678 in *Bufton's Diary*.[2] Mr. King finds mention in ancient deeds of a SWAN —either inn, shop, or tenement—at Prittlewell in 1652. In the *Records of the House of Gurney* (p. 539) there is mention of " a messuage or tenement heretofore called or known by the name or sign of the SWAN, situate in the parish of St. Mary, Maldon," in the seventeenth century. Perhaps the *SWAN Inn still existing in the High Street is the same house. In 1678 there was a BLACK SWAN at or near Audley End. Poor Robin (see p. 66) mentions it in his *Perambulation from Saffron Walden to London*. After his acquaintances had drunk heavily with him at the ROSE AND CROWN, Saffron Walden, whence he started, he says—

> " Yet would my jovial friends on me attend,
> Part of my Journey unto Audley End,
> By them called Ninevah, but no great city,
> Though too much sin may be there, more's the pity.
> There at the sign (of such a thing, I think,
> As never swam on pond or river's brink)
> Of a Black Swan, I entered in.
>
> .   .   .   .   .   .
>
> Yet although of this sign there's no such thing,
> It was a sign there was good drink within."

---

[1] Dale's *Annals of Coggeshall*, p. 160.   [2] Ibid. p. 261.

Of the well-known OLD FOUR SWANS at Waltham Cross Mr. E. Walford, in *Greater London* (vol. i. p. 393), writes as follows :—

"It is undoubtedly an old building ; but it is questionable whether it can properly lay claim to the antiquity that is locally assigned to it ; for in it, according to tradition, the body of Queen Eleanor remained for the night preceding its solemn entry into London. Salmon considers this inn to have been the original manor-house of the honour of Richmond ; and Gough says that it 'bears marks of great antiquity in the forms of its chimneys, and the quantity of chestnut timber employed about it.' A large signboard, supported on tall posts, placed on the opposite sides of the way, swings across the road, having on it the inscription, 'Ye Olde Foure Swannes Hostelrie, 1260.' "

David Hughson, in his work on *London* (vol. ii. p. 339), says of this house, that in 1805 it was a good specimen of the old style of house, "consisting of three sides, sometimes of four, with an entrance by a square aperture in the front, into the quadrangle. . . . It is the manor-house of the manor of Theobalds, and was formerly the residence of a natural son of Henry VIII., whom he created Earl of Richmond." In the parish register of Waltham Holy Cross, or Waltham Abbey, there is the following entry : "Julii, 1612, Margarett, the daughter of Edward Scarlett of Cestrehunt, was buried 26 daye, dwelling at the signe of Ye Old Swanne in Waltham Cross." In days gone by this inn was a well-known posting-house, and more recently it numbered Charles Lamb among its patrons. The SWAN WITH TWO NECKS was formerly the sign of a private house in Head Street, Colchester, once occupied by Miles Gray, the celebrated bell-founder. In his day he was quite the head of his craft. Bells founded either by him or his son and successor Miles, who died in 1686, are still found in many belfries throughout Essex. In his will, dated May 17, 1649,[1] he bequeaths unto his wife Dorothy all the " rents, issues, p'fits, cominge, growinge, and arisinge out of the east end of the capitall messuage or tenement, lately burned downe, scituate and beinge below Head Gate, in Colchester aforesayd, commonly called or knowne by the

[1] *Vide Trans. Essex Arch. Soc.*, N. S., vol. iii. part i. p. 74.

name of the Swann wth two Neckes," &c. It is commonly
supposed that the word "necks" has been corrupted from
"nicks," swans having formerly been marked by nicks or
notches on the bill. The Rev. Stephen Weston, in the
Archæologia for 1812, states that the king's swans were
formerly marked by *two nicks*, as shown in the two illustrations
given below, which represent the royal swan-marks of Henry
VIII. and Edward IV. respectively. These, he says, were
not afterwards understood, and the double-headed two-
necked swan was invented. Larwood and Hotten, however,
doubt this derivation, chiefly because the nicks would have
been so small when represented on the sign-board as to be
of no practical use as a distinctive sign.

The Cock is a very ancient and very common sign. Lar-

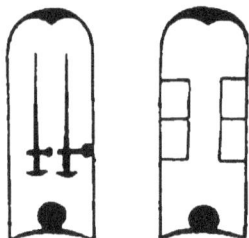

SWAN BILLS WITH TWO NICKS.
(*After Yarrell.*)

SWAN WITH TWO NECKS.
(*After Larwood and Hotten.*)

wood and Hotten say that it was already in use in the time
of the Romans. We have no less than eighteen examples
of the simple Cock, and an Old Cock occurs at Sheering.
The ancient and well-known Cock Hotel at Epping finds
frequent mention in the numbers of the *Chelmsford Chronicle*
for the year 1786. Taylor (see p. 28) also mentions it by
name as long ago as 1636. It is a very old house, though
now re-fronted with brick. The Rev. Wm. Cole, in his
voluminous MSS. in the British Museum, says that on the
26th of October, 1774, he "arrived at Epping in the dusk
of the evening, and lodged and dined late at the Cock Inn."
The Cock Inn still existing at Stock is several times mentioned in the parish registers, namely, in 1634, 1639, and
1693. On the latter occasion, "a stranger who died at the

Cock, being a poor man, was buried by the constables, November 20." The COCKE Inn at Great Coggeshall (not now existing) was once a house of good standing. In 1614 James I. granted it to Henry Eades, and in 1616 to Peregrine Gastrell and Ralph Lounds.[1] Not improbably in this case the sign was derived from the arms of the Abbey of Coggeshall.[2] The COCK, near the Church at Waltham Abbey, is a very ancient inn. It finds frequent mention in the old parish registers. The marriage of John Broadly, of the COCK Inn, is recorded as early as February, 1599. In 1662 there was a COCK at Chelmsford, which does not appear to be in existence now. It is mentioned as being "on the hither side of the bridge" (*i.e.*, the side nearest to Romford) in the *Account of the Murder of Thomas Kidderminster*, already referred to. This was probably the same inn mentioned by Foxe in his *Book of Martyrs* when he says that "one Richard Potto the elder, an inn-holder, dwelling at the sign of the Cocke, did much trouble" George Eagles, who was martyred in 1557. For the prevalence of this sign we have probably to thank the barbarous old custom of cock-fighting, as is obvious in the case of the sign of the FIGHTING COCKS, which occurs at Little Sampford and Wendens Ambo, and the GAME COCK at Chadwell Heath. But the cock is also by no means an uncommon heraldic bearing, and several combinations into which the bird enters have probably had an heraldic origin. For instance, the sign of the COCK AND CROWN, which existed at Colchester forty years back, may have represented one of the badges of Henry VIII., which was a *white cock crowned, with the cypher H.R.* The same king also often used a *white cock crowned*, as one of his supporters. At the same time it may simply have been an impaled sign of very modern date. In any case it is very rare. The COCK AND BELL, which appears at High Easter, Writtle, and *Romford, is an apparently meaningless sign, and is probably an impalement. The last-named example seems, however, to have been in existence for at least a century, as it is mentioned in an advertisement in the

[1] Dale's *Annals of Coggeshall*, p. 79.   [2] Three Cocks.

Chelmsford Chronicle for September 14, 1764. In Wright's
History of Essex the inn itself is depicted. Taylor, too, probably refers to this house in his *Catalogue of Tavernes* when
he mentions a COCK at Romford in 1636. The example at
Writtle has an old pictorial sign-board representing a re-
splendent, though faded, cock, with a bell over his head.
The COCK AND MAGPIE, which has existed since 1789 at
least on Epping Green, is probably called after a celebrated
London tavern of the same name. The sign is identical in
its origin with that of the COCK AND PIE. By the latter
name is known some wine and spirit vaults of repute which
for over a century have been established on *North Hill,
Colchester. Several more or less likely meanings for the
sign have been suggested, but the authors of the *History of
Sign-boards* consider it to be a corrupted sign. They believe
that it originally represented the PEACOCK PIE, formerly
a very favourite dish. When the dish went out of fashion
the sign became abbreviated into the COCK AND PIE ; and as
that appeared meaningless, it was in time corrupted into the
COCK AND MAGPIE, in both of which forms we still have it.
Forty years ago the sign of the MAGPIE existed at Great
Warley, and there is now a PEACOCK at Canning Town. A
rebus upon the name of the issuer, Richard Cock of Colchester, occurs on a farthing token dated 1658. The RAVEN
as a sign is found at Berden. It was a badge of the old
Scotch kings, and may have been set up as a Jacobite
symbol. The BLACKBIRDS, which occurs at Bulmer, and
the THREE BLACKBIRDS, which occurs at Leyton, are, doubtless, two signs which were identical in their origin, and are
probably connected with the RAVEN, the THREE RAVENS,
the THREE CROWS, and the THREE CHOUGHS, all of which
are fairly common in other counties, and are supposed by
Larwood and Hotten to typify Charles, James, and Rupert.
It is, however, just as likely that they represent the modern
version of some family coat of arms. Many such coats bear
three birds, which might, with almost equal correctness, be
referred to any of the species just mentioned. Various doves
and pigeons have already been spoken of (p. 38), but there

still remains to be mentioned the curious sign of the RAINBOW AND DOVE, which is to be found at North Weald. In the list of signs in 1789 (p. 7) it appears as the RAINBOW merely. The sign is apparently quite meaningless, unless it typifies the rainbow and dove which figure in the account of "the Flood" (Genesis, chaps. viii. and ix.). The NIGHTIN- GALE at Wanstead is another inn-sign which does not seem to be mentioned by Larwood and Hotten. It is at least forty years old, and, doubtless, takes its name from, or gives its name to, Nightingale Square, in which it stands. The sign of the OWL, which has existed at High Beech since 1789 at least, is spoken of in the *History of Sign-boards* as occurring only once elsewhere, namely, at Calverley, near Leeds. A bird (presumably a FINCH) occurs on the halfpenny token of John Finch of Halstead, who was probably a maltster, as the other side of his token bore the representation of a MALT-SCOOP. The BIRD IN HAND occurs five times in Essex, namely, at Braintree, Halstead (twice), Coggeshall, and *Stratford. There are also beer-houses so called at Goldhanger and Chelmsford. Mr. G. F. Beaumont of Coggeshall states that the *BIRD IN HAND at that place was formerly known as the THOROUGH Inn, because there was a right of way or thoroughfare through it from Earl Street to Church Street. He also mentions, as a curious coincidence, that a short time since the name of the tenant was Joseph *Bird*, and that of the owner Richard *Bird* Holmes. The same gentleman contributes to the *Coggeshall Almanac* for the present year an interesting " Programme of a Procession, exhibited by the Weavers of Coggeshall, on Wednesday, the 15th of June, 1791," and which was to "set out precisely at eight o'clock from the BIRD IN HAND." The idea of the sign is suggested by the proverb—

> "A bird in hand is better far,
> Than two that in the bushes are."

The device is to be seen on some of the trade tokens of the seventeenth century. The sign of the FEATHERS at Hatfield Broad Oak is clearly identical with that of the PLUME OF FEATHERS at Loughton; indeed, the former appears in Mr. Creed's list (p. 7) as having been the PLUME OF FEATHERS in 1789. The house at Loughton is also mentioned in the same list, so that both are at least a hundred years old. Both, of course, now at least represent the badge of our Princes of Wales. Ostrich feathers have been among the devices of our kings and princes from very early times; and the pretty tale of how the Black Prince took them from the King of Bohemia, whom he killed in the battle of Creci, is a pure delusion. As the Rev. H. L. Elliot points out, "Single feathers, differenced in various ways, were used as badges by the kings and the Beauforts before the Wars of the Roses. Henry VI. used two feathers in saltire, the sinister argent, surmounted of the dexter or, as here depicted, as one of his badges."

PLUME OF FEATHERS.
(*Badge of the Prince of Wales.*)

THE FEATHERS.
(*Badge of Henry VI.*)

Twenty years since a house at Stanstead bore the sign of the BELL AND FEATHERS, which is a combination not mentioned by Larwood and Hotten. It was probably merely an impaled sign, as it was formerly the BELL simply, and has now returned to its old name, under which it will be hereafter referred to. The sign of the PHŒNIX now only occurs at Rainham, though there was another example at Billericay forty years since. The sign was formerly often set up by chemists, but other tradesmen also used it. The fact that a phœnix forms the crest of the Blacksmiths' Company (p. 32) has, perhaps, had something to do with bringing the bird into favour as a sign. This completes our list of ornithological signs.

CHAPTER V.

PISCATORY, INSECT, AND REPTILIAN SIGNS.

. . . "Ye ale-house painted signs."
SHAKESPEARE: *Titus Andronicus*, Act iv., Scene 3.

THIS class of signs—or rather combination of several small groups, taken together for the sake of convenience—is, naturally, very far from a large one. It contains, indeed, only four signs, all told.

The FISH AND EELS, which is a very strange device appearing at Roydon, is our only existing sign connected with fish, although TWO FISHES appeared on the tokens of the two William Wildmans (father and son) of Saffron Walden, issued in 1656 and 1667 respectively. The former spells the name Saffron Wallding. The sign, perhaps, originated in the arms of the Fishmongers' Company.[1] Larwood and Hotten do not notice the Fish and Eels, although this house has displayed the sign since 1789 at least. It may be a meaningless impalement.

Only two signs occurring in the county are in any way connected with insects. These are the FLY AND BULLOCK, already described (p. 67), and the BEEHIVE, which occurs five times, namely, at Great Baddow, Witham, Horkesley, Ilford, and Lambourne. The sign is generally represented (as at Witham and Baddow) by an old straw hive, or skep, with a great many bees, *volant, counter-volant* (as heraldic

---

[1] Azure ; three crowned dolphins in pale between two pairs of crowned lucies saltire ; on a chief, three pairs of keys in saltire.

writers say), around it, probably to indicate that a busy trade is carried on within. It is recorded [1] in the Barking parish register, that in 1653, " Francis, the sonne of an Ethiopian, born at the BEEHIVE," was baptised. Under this heading must be noticed a sign which, although it does not occur in Essex, is, nevertheless, connected with the county. This sign is the ESSEX SERPENT, which still exists in King Street, Covent Garden ; and, when Larwood and Hotten wrote, there was also another example in Charles Street, Westminster. Those gentlemen think that it was, perhaps, originally set up " in allusion to a fabulous monster recorded in a catalogue of wonders and awful prognostications contained in a broadside of 1704,[2] from which we learn that ' Before Henry the second dyed, . . . a Dragon of marvellous bigness was discovered at St. Osyph in Essex.' Had we any evidence that it is an old sign, we might almost be inclined to consider it as dating from the civil war, and hung up with reference to Essex, the Parliamentary General ; for, though we have searched the chroniclers fondest of relating wonders and monstrous apparitions, we have not succeeded in finding any authority for the St. Osyph Dragon, other than the above-mentioned broadside." Another reference to the same unwelcome visitor is, however, to be found in Dr. Howell's *Ancient and Present State of England* (1712), wherein it is recorded (p. 75) that " At St. Osyphs in Essex was seen a dragon of marvellous bigness, which by moving burned houses." The dragon is also mentioned in Sir Richard Baker's *Chronicles of the Kings of England*, published in 1684. It is, nevertheless, fairly certain that the sign has no reference to the St. Osyth dragon ; for there is a much more likely origin. In the British Museum Library may be seen a highly remarkable tract of the year 1669, entitled, *The Flying Serpent, or Strange News out of Essex : being a true relation of a Monstrous Serpent which hath divers times been seen at a parish called Henham on the Mount, within four miles of Saffron Walden. Showing the length, proportion, and bigness of the Ser-*

---

[1] *Trans. Essex Arch. Soc.*, vol. ii. p. 128.
[2] Reprinted in *Notes and Queries* for January 15, 1859.

pent, the place where it commonly lurks, and what means hath been

THE FLYING SERPENT.
(*Facsimile of Original.*)

used to kill it. Also a discourse of other Serpents, and particularly

of a Cockatrice killed at Saffron Walden," &c.[1]   The truth of
the statements contained in the tract is attested by the
Churchwarden, the Constable, the Overseer of the Poor, and
four Householders.   The title-page bears no author's name,
and the imprint of the copy in question is partially destroyed ;
but there can be little doubt that it is one of the many curious
productions of " Poor Robin," whose *Perambulation from
Saffron Walden to London* has already been noticed (p. 66).[2]
In addition to an awe-inspiring portrait of the beast, here
reproduced, the tract contains a very amusing, though now
highly absurd, account of the first discovery of the serpent,
the nature of its habitat, the means taken to kill it,
and other details, as set forth in the title.   Doubtless the
appearance of the tract caused sufficient talk and attracted
enough attention to induce some enterprising publican or
other tradesman to set up the ESSEX SERPENT as a sign ; or
perhaps some former GRIFFIN or GREEN DRAGON was re-
christened under that name in order to attract customers.
That it is a fairly old sign is certain.   Gough, in his *British
Topography*,[3] after alluding to the pamphlet just spoken of,
says : " Mr. Oldys [who died in 1761] says there is a public-
house in King Street, Covent Garden, called the Essex
Serpent, and having a serpent painted on its sign."   Sussex
had a " strange and monstrous Serpent (or Dragon) " in 1614,
as may be learned from a very curious old pamphlet of that
date, entitled *True and Wonderful*, republished in the *Harleian
Miscellany*.[4]   Essex can boast of a reptilian sign which probably exists nowhere else, a beer-house keeper at Ingatestone
having, for some inscrutable reason, selected the VIPER—a
device not noticed by Larwood and Hotten.

[1] This amusing and curious tract has since been reproduced in facsimile, illustration and all, with an introduction by the author of this
work.   It may be obtained from Mr. Wm. Masland, Bookseller, of Saffron
Walden, price 6d.

[2] See a list of many of his effusions, by Mr. H. Ecroyd Smith, in
Notes and Queries for April 28, 1883 (p. 321).

[3] 1780, vol. i. p. 355.   [4] Vol. iii. p. 109.

CHAPTER VI.

BOTANICAL SIGNS.

HE next great class of signs which will be noticed includes those which are derived from the Vegetable Kingdom. These may be called "Botanical Signs." Though not so numerous as the Zoological Signs, they are, nevertheless, fairly common; but only a comparatively small number can be traced back to an heraldic origin.

Those signs will be noticed first which are obviously derived from some prominent tree or trees growing close to the houses called after them. These seem generally to be of very modern origin, as they figure but sparsely in the list printed forty years ago. Most of them, it will be noticed, are in the vicinity of London. There is a BAY TREE at Stratford, a CHESTNUT TREE at Walthamstow, an ELMS at Leytonstone, a FIR TREES at Wanstead, a FOUR ASHES at Takeley, a GROVE Tavern at Walthamstow, a HOLLY BUSH at Leyton, and another at Loughton, a HOLLY TREE at Forest Gate, and a MAY BUSH at Great Oakley. The sign of the WILLOWS appears at Willingale Doe. There is also on the list a THREE ASHES at Cressing, and another at Chelmsford, while forty years since there was another at Rochford, a YEW TREE at Great Horkesley, and another at Felstead (beer-house), a THREE ELMS at Chignal St. James (which has three elm trees in front of it), and no less than seven CHERRY TREES in different parts of the county, although forty years ago only four were in existence. The

THORN INN at *Mistley seems to have been in existence since 1786 at least, as it is mentioned in an advertisement in the *Chelmsford Chronicle* for February 24th in that year. Its sign is, obviously, connected with the old name of the place, which was Mistley Thorn. In the *Very Young Lady's Tour from London to Aldborough and Back* (1804, see p. 37) occurs the following :

> "Our first stage is to Mistley ; we stop at the Thorn,
> And shall see the fine sights which that village adorn."

There is a ROUND BUSH (beer-shop) at Purleigh. At Havering there is an ORANGE TREE, and in the *Cattle Market at Braintree there is another house with the same name. The latter has been in existence for at least forty years. At Chelmsford, too, near the New London Road, there is a beer-shop known as the ORANGE TREE. Inquiry has shown that the house was built some years ago by a woman who had saved sufficient money for the purpose out of dealing in oranges. She named her beer-shop the ORANGE TREE, a name which it has since retained, though it has long since passed out of her hands. There are WALNUT TREES at Little Horkesley and Great Waltham (beer-house). In 1662 there was another house of the same name at "Mile-end Green" (probably Mill Green, Writtle, or Mile End Green, Great Easton), as mentioned in the *Account of the Murder of Thomas Kidderminster*, already referred to (p. 56). There is some doubt as to whether or not the sign of the OAK, which occurs three times, namely, at Halstead, Messing, and Great Saling, and that of the OLD OAK, which occurs at Romford, ought to be included in this catalogue. These signs may be, and probably are, identical with that of the ROYAL OAK, which occurs eighteen times in different parts of the county, and of course commemorates the incident of King Charles II. hiding in an oak tree, though it is certainly strange that this comparatively trivial incident should have continued to be so long and so frequently commemorated. It is also a very common beer-house sign. The OAK, too, is put to the same

use at Braintree. The following very unpoetical production,
by H. Jopson, the landlord, is displayed in the tap-room of
the ROYAL OAK at Saffron Walden :

> "As customers come, and I do trust them,
> I lose my money, likewise my custom ;
> Though chalk is cheap, say what you will,
> Chalk won't pay the brewer's bill ;
> So I must try to keep a decent tap,
> For ready-money and no strap."

The THEYDON OAK at Theydon Garnon until last year bore
upon one side of its sign-board a very good representation
of the fine old oak from which it takes its name, and close to
which it stands. The KING'S OAK at High Beech is a sign
which is probably quite distinct from the ROYAL OAK. The
author of *Nooks and Corners in Essex* says that the house
takes its name "from an old stump near thereto, formerly
called Harold's Oak." This, however, is probably an error,
as the large old oak which stands on the green before the
house has long been known as the " King's Oak." Local
tradition says that Henry VIII., while hunting in the forest
on the day on which Ann Boleyn was beheaded, rested under
this tree while waiting to hear the gun, fired from the Tower,
which announced the death of the Queen. Other localities
also claim the oak under which the king listened, but this is
as likely as any other to be the right one. The KING'S OAK
is marked on Cary's *Map of Fifteen Miles round London* (1786),
and also on Andrew and Drury's *Map of Essex* (1777). There
was formerly an OAKS in Stifford. It now serves as three
cottages, standing opposite the school. At it, in the beginning of last century, the churchwardens treated themselves
to costly dinners. In 1712, for instance, the records in the
parish chest inform us that the " vestory stood adjourned "
to the OAKS. A TREE occurs upon the farthing token of
" W. Spiltimber of Hatfild Broad Oake," doubtless in
allusion both to the name of the issuer and to the old oak,
commonly called the " Doodle Oak," from which the village
takes its name. At the same place a beer-house is still
known as the DOODLE OAK.

A public-house on Shenfield Common has, for at least forty years, borne the sign of the ARTICHOKE. This is one of the very last productions of the vegetable kingdom which one would expect to find represented upon a sign-board ; but Larwood and Hotten, who think it originally found a place there when first introduced, say that " it used to be a great favourite, and still gives name to some public-houses." Another very extraordinary sign, unnoticed in the *History of Sign-boards*, is the CAULIFLOWER, which appears at Great Ilford. Unless due merely to a landlord's caprice, it is difficult to suggest any possible origin for it. The present landlord, in whose family the house has been for 120 years, can give no information about the matter, further than that the existing house was built forty-eight years ago, the old inn having been pulled down to make room for the railway. There is also a beer-house so called at Rainham. Of the BUSH, which, according to Larwood and Hotten (p. 4), " must certainly be counted amongst the most ancient and popular of signs," Essex does not appear to have a single example. The same authorities elsewhere (p. 233) declare it to be " the oldest sign borrowed from the vegetable kingdom," and state that it came originally from the Romans, together with the common saying, " Good wine needs no bush." As late as the reign of James I. many inns used it as their sign. At Bardfield, and probably other towns in the county, houses specially licensed for the sale of liquor at fair time still fasten branches of oak and other trees to their fronts as a sign, a custom which is not unknown in other parts of the country. It is without doubt a modern form of the ancient sign of the BUSH. It appears, too, in every way probable that the curious besom-like ornaments so often to be seen upon the ends of old sign-irons are also conventional representations of the same venerable device. Examples are to be seen in the drawings of the sign-irons of the SIX BELLS at Dunmow (p. 168), and the SUGAR LOAVES at Sible Hedingham (p. 39). At Theydon Garnon there is a beer-house called the GARNON BUSHES, so named doubtless after a part of Epping Forest, which goes by that name. At Hornchurch there is a beer-shop known as the FURZE, probable a unique sign. The TULIP at Springfield appears to be also unique. Possibly the landlord who adopted the sign was a cultivator of tulips.

The BARLEY Mow, meaning a barley stack, is an ancient sign which still occurs at Stanstead and at *Colchester. Doubtless it was first put up as a sign in honour of John Barleycorn, just as the VINE, which occurs at Great Bardfield and Black Notley (beer-house), and the GRAPES, which occurs at Colchester (the latter being still the recognized sign of a vintner), both undoubtedly found a place on the sign-board because they helped to supply the wherewithal for the worship of Bacchus. Forty years since there was another VINE Inn at Thaxted. The HOP-POLE, which is a sign occurring at Good Easter, and the HOP-POLES, which is another occurring at Great Hallingbury, both obviously found their place on the sign-board for the same reason. There are also beer-houses with the sign of the HOP-POLES at Little Hallingbury and Roydon, although the cultivation of hops has now ceased at those places. Hop-growing once flourished extensively in Essex, and these two signs are relics of the now almost relinquished industry. At the beginning of this century they were grown at the Hedinghams, the Maplesteads, the Colnes, Halstead, Wethersfield, Finchingfield, Great Bardfield, and Shalford, as well as at Moulsham, Good Easter, Roxwell, Chignal St. James, and other places round Chelmsford. Fifty years earlier the cultivation of hops in the county was spread over a wider area, though the number of acres grown was about the same. At the present time the cultivation is all but discontinued. Until the year 1883 there was a hop-ground adjoining Skreen's Park, Roxwell, but it is now devoted to other purposes. Round the Hedinghams, however, hops are still grown, their cultivation having been introduced by a former Mr. Majendie in 1792. Daniel Defoe says, in his *Tour through Great Britain,* that in 1724, hops were brought direct from Chelmsford for sale at the great Stourbridge Hop Fair.

The description of the MAYPOLE at Chigwell, given by Dickens in *Barnaby Rudge*, will occur to every one.   It runs as follows :—

" In the year 1775, there stood upon the Borders of Epping Forest, at a distance of about twelve miles from London—measuring from the standard in Cornhill, or rather from the spot on or near to which the standard used to be in days of yore—a house of public entertainment called the Maypole ; which fact was demonstrated to all such travellers as could neither read nor write (and sixty-six years ago a vast number, both of travellers and stay-at-homes, were in this condition) by the emblem reared on the roadside over against the house, which, if not of those goodly proportions that maypoles were wont to present in olden times, was a fair young ash, thirty feet in height, and as straight as any arrow that ever English yeoman drew.

" The Maypole—by which term henceforth is meant the house and not its sign—the Maypole was an old building, with more gable ends than a lazy man would care to count on a sunny day ; huge zig-zag chimneys, out of which it seemed as though even smoke could not choose but come in more than naturally fantastic shapes, imparted to it in its tortuous progress ; and vast stables, gloomy, ruinous, and empty.   The place was said to have been built in the days of King Henry the Eighth ; and there was a legend not only that Queen Elizabeth had slept there one night while upon a hunting excursion, to wit in a certain oak panelled room with a deep bay-window, but that next morning, while standing on a mounting-block before the door with one foot in the stirrup, the virgin monarch had then and there boxed and cuffed an unlucky page for some neglect of duty.   The matter-of-fact and doubtful folks, of whom there were a few among the Maypole customers, as unluckily there always are in every little community, were inclined to look upon this tradition as rather apocryphal ; but, whenever the landlord of that ancient hostelry appealed to the mounting-block itself as evidence, and triumphantly pointed out that there it stood in the same place to that very day, the doubters never failed to be put down by a large majority, and all true believers exulted, as in a victory.

" Whether these, and many other stories of the like nature, were true or untrue, the Maypole was really an old house, a very old house, perhaps as old as it claimed to be, and perhaps older, which will sometimes happen with houses of an uncertain, as with ladies of a certain, age.   Its windows were all diamond-pane lattices, its-floors were sunken and uneven, its ceilings blackened by the hand of time and heavy with massive beams.   Over the doorway was an ancient porch, quaintly and grotesquely carved ; and here on summer evenings the more favoured customers smoked and drank—ay, and sang many a good song too, sometimes—reposing on two grim-looking high-backed settles, which, like the twin dragons of some fairy tale, guarded the entrance to the mansion.

" In the chimneys of the disused rooms, swallows had built their nests for many a long year, and from earliest spring to latest autumn whole colonies of sparrows chirped and twittered in the eaves.   There were more pigeons about the dreary stable-yard and outbuildings than anybody but the landlord could reckon up.   The wheeling and circling flights of runts, fantails, tumblers, and pouters, were perhaps not quite consistent with the grave and sober character of the building, but the monotonous cooing, which never ceased to be raised by some among them all day long, suited it exactly, and seemed to lull it to rest. With its overhanging storys, drowsy little panes of glass, and front bulging out and projecting over the pathway, the old house looked as if it were nodding in its sleep. Indeed it needed no very great stretch of fancy to detect in it other resemblances to humanity. The bricks of which it was built had originally been a deep dark red, but had grown yellow and discoloured like an old man's skin ; the sturdy timbers had decayed like teeth ; and here and there the ivy, like a warm garment to comfort it in its age, wrapped its green leaves closely round the time-worn walls.

"It was a hale and hearty age, though, still ; and in the summer or autumn evenings, when the glow of the setting sun fell upon the oak and chestnut trees of the adjacent forest, the old house, partaking of its lustre, seemed their fit companion, and to have many good years of life in him yet."

The house indicated in the foregoing description still stands, much as it was in the days of which Dickens wrote. It is, however, *not* the MAYPOLE at Chigwell. Dickens, to suit the purposes of his tale, made free use of that license usually allowed to poets and writers of fiction. His description, as above, gives a very fair idea of the fine old hostelry known as the KING'S HEAD, situate opposite the church in the village of Chigwell, where it has displayed the same sign since 1789 at least. It was in what has since been known as the " Chester Room " in this house, that a portion, at least, of *Barnaby Rudge* was penned. On the sign-board swinging over the door, there is a large portrait of King Charles I., painted some years ago by Miss Herring. At Chigwell Row, about two miles distant, there *is* a MAYPOLE INN, with a maypole still before the door, and on the site which Dickens indicates ; but the foregoing description is (as has been said) that of the KING'S HEAD. The present MAYPOLE is an inn of no special pretensions, and is not the same house that displayed the sign at least as early as 1789. A writer in *Notes and Queries*,[1] says that the following was formerly to be seen on the sign :—

| "My liquor's good, | Excuse me, sirs, |
| My measure's just, | I cannot trust." |

---

[1] First Series, vol. x. p. 32.

KING'S HEAD INN.
(*At Chigwell.*)

Over the fireplace was seen these lines:—

"All you who stand   That other folks
   Before the fire,   As well as you
  I pray sit down.   May see the fire
   It's my desire   And feel it too."

An inscription upon the stable-door ran as follows:—

"Whoever smokes tobacco here,
Shall forfeit sixpence to spend in beer.
Your pipes lay by when you come here,
Or fire to me may prove severe."

The only other sign of the kind now to be seen in Essex is the OLD MAYPOLE at Barkingside. Andrews and Drury's *Map of Essex*, however, published in 1777, shows houses with this sign then existing at Chigwell, Barking, and Collier's Row. A writer in the *Gentleman's Magazine*, speaking of Maypoles, says, "The last in London was taken down in 1717, and removed to Wanstead in Essex. It was more than 100 feet high, and stood on the east side of Somerset House." The custom of celebrating Mayday has now almost died out in the county, except at Saffron Walden, where, every "Garland Day," it is customary to see the High Street of the town crowded during the morning with children, each bearing a "garland" more or less tastefully arranged upon a hoop, or in some other way. They diligently visit all the houses asking for coppers, which are generally given with liberality. The WHEATSHEAF, as already stated (p. 33), appears as a sign no less than seven times in Essex. Wheatsheaves form charges on the arms of at least three of the great Trade Companies, namely, the Brewers' (p. 32), the Bakers' (p. 33), and the Inn-holders'.[1] Although the sign of the BAKERS' ARMS now only occurs once in Essex, two tokens issued in Chelmsford, one issued in Braintree, and several issued in Colchester, bear the arms of the Bakers' Company; and as there are now houses displaying the sign of the WHEATSHEAF in each of those places, and all of them have existed for at

[1] Azure ; a chevron, per pale and per chevron, gules and argent counterchanged, between three garbs or ; on a chief argent, a St. Julian's cross sable.

least forty years, it is quite possible that they are the same establishments kept, two centuries ago, by the issuers of the tokens. As a beer-house sign, too, the WHEATSHEAF is still common.

The CROWN AND THISTLE, which occurs at Great Chesterford, is a rather uncommon sign. It, of course, represents the royal badge of Scotland, *a thistle, imperially crowned.*

Few will be surprised to learn that the ROSE is very common as a sign. A rose imperially crowned is now the national badge of England; white and red roses formed the cognizances of the rival factions of York and Lancaster in the " Wars of the Roses;" the same flower, under different forms, served as the badge of nearly all the English sovereigns from Edward I. to Anne; and it is one of the very commonest "vegetable" charges known in Heraldry. The fact that, while the sign of a simple ROSE occurs only three times in Essex, namely, at Southchurch, Peldon, and West Mersea, the ROSE AND CROWN occurs as many as twenty-five times, clearly shows the heraldic origin of the sign, most of our kings and queens having worn the rose crowned. The Rose

ROSE AND THISTLE.
(Badge of James I.)

and the Thistle combined together in a very absurd heraldic style, and crowned, were used as a badge by James I. to typify the union of the two kingdoms of England and Scotland. On the beautiful chapel of Henry VII. at Cambridge the rose and crown are repeated innumerable times, together with the king's other badges, a portcullis and a fleur-de-lys, both of them crowned. A rose crowned also appears on the token of "Iohn Freeherne iunior, in Witham, 1667." The authors of the *History of Sign-boards* say (p. 124): "Hutton, in his *Battle of Bosworth*, says that ' upon the death of Richard III., and consequent overthrow of the York Faction, all the signboards with white roses were pulled down, and none are to be found at the present day.' This last part of the statement, we

believe, is true." The rose in the sign of the ROSE AND CROWN
at Thaxted is, nevertheless, painted white, though this is
certainly unusual. On Cary's and other old maps of Essex,
published about a century ago, may be seen marked two houses,
presumably inns, known as the WHITE ROSE and the RED
ROSE, situated near one another on the edge of Epping Forest.
Neither of these signs appear in Essex at the present day, nor
do Larwood and Hotten mention them. There is also a WHITE
ROSE in Castle Street, Leicester Square, London. The ROSE
AND CROWN at Saffron Walden has long been the principal
inn in the town. One of the earliest references to it in the
Corporation records occurs in 1654, when 2s. were expended
" For 1 Quart of canary at the Rose when Moulton and
Douglas suffered." In 1660, 2s. 4d. was " Spent at the Rose
and Crown when Captain Turner sent about the town
armes." In the following year, and again in 1682, the name
appears again ; while in the years 1689, 1704, 1709, and 1819,
the Corporation seems to have expended various sums at " the
ROSE " (undoubtedly the same house) upon certain special
occasions. It was from this house, too, that " Poor Robin "
started on his *Perambulation from Saffron Walden to London*
in 1678 (see p. 66), as shown by the following extracts. He
says :—

>   .   .   .   .
>
> " Thus, having shown you *when*, in the next place
> I'll show you *whence*, my journey I did trace.
>
>   .   .   .   .   .   .
>
> It was from the Rose and Crown, where Mr. Eve
> Doth keep a house like to an Under Sheriff ;
> There is good Sack, good French wine and good Beer.
>
>   .   .   .   .   .
>
> There, at my parting, some kind friends of mine,
> Would needs bestow on me a quart of wine,
> Where, with stout drinking, ere my parting hour,
> That quart was made at least a three or four.
> Yet would my jovial friends on me attend,
> Part of my journey unto Audley End."

The Mr. Eve mentioned herein is undoubtedly the same
landlord mentioned in the Saffron Walden *Mayor's Book*
in 1680, when the Corporation " Pd. Mr. Eves for wine at

the Dinner, &c., when the King came to Audley End, when we delivered the Address—£5 2s. od." The ROSE at Peldon appears to be at least a century old, as it is mentioned in the *Chelmsford Chronicle* on May 5, 1786. The inn plays a

ROSE INN AT PELDON (after the earthquake).

rather conspicuous part in the Rev. Baring-Gould's *Mehalah,* wherein (ii. p. 58) it is described as " an old-fashioned house with a vine scrambling over the red tile roof, and an ancient standard sign on the green before the door, bearing a rose painted the size of a gigantic turnip." Few houses suffered more severely from the earthquake of April 22, 1884, than this. An illustration of its appearance immediately after that event is here given.

Mr. King finds mention in ancient deeds of a ROSE AND CROWN—either inn, shop, or tenement—at Rochford in 1693. In the Stock parish registers it is recorded that on August 23, 1676, " Richard Barnes, a citizen of London, dwelling (as he sayd) in the Minories, taken sick in travell, dyed in yᵉ highway neare yᵉ house called yᵉ Rose, and was burried at yᵉ p'ishes charge." Presumably this ROSE was not an inn. A ROSE appears on the token, dated 1670, of Thomas Guyon of Coggeshall, but no house with that sign now exists there. The ROSE AND CROWN at Rochford is referred to in the *Chelmsford Chronicle* on April 14, 1786. The sign of the ROSE OF DENMARK occurs at Canning Town. Its origin is not obvious. Larwood and Hotten do not refer to the sign.

CHAPTER VII.

HUMAN SIGNS.

. . . "And make my image but an ale-house sign."
SHAKESPEARE: HENRY V., Part II., Act iii., Scene 2.

HE next class of signs to be treated of is that which includes those derived from "Man and His Parts," as the old books on Heraldry have it. Such signs may be styled "Human Signs." They are numerous, though usually of but very slight interest; and, as might be expected, very few are of heraldic origin. In speaking of them it will not be necessary to give much more than a mere list. The numerous "heads" obviously indicate a portrait once to have been the sign; and most of these portraits represent persons of very modern fame. Many Human Signs have already been noticed under the heading "Arms," and elsewhere, and it will be quite unnecessary to refer to them again.

By no means a few of our inns are named after personages who have made themselves eminent either in the political, military, literary, or social worlds. The mere mention of these will call to mind many historical events of importance during the last two centuries. Thus our six examples of the DUKE OF WELLINGTON, our two of the WELLINGTON, and our six of the DUKE'S HEAD, remind us of the hero of Talavera and Salamanca—*the* Duke of his day—who died in 1852. A DUKE'S HEAD, however, which existed at Hatfield Broad Oak in 1789, evidently commemorated some other and earlier Duke, perhaps one of the Dukes of York. There is also a DUKE OF WELLINGTON (beer-house) at Bocking. The ADMIRAL ROUS at Galleywood, where Chelmsford Races are held, commemorates the father of modern English racing, who died only a year or two ago. The OLIVER TWIST at Leyton was doubtless set up in honour of the popular Dickens, who well deserves further sign-board · honours. The same may be said of another great Englishman, who is commemorated only by the SHAKESPEARE'S HEAD at Canning Town. In various parts of the county we meet with two examples of the EARL OF ESSEX, one of the DUKE OF NORFOLK, three of the GROSVENOR, one of the LORD HENNIKER, and one of the CLIFTON, all of which were unquestionably set up in honour of great titled families. Statesmen are represented by two examples of the EARL OF DERBY, one of the LORD STANLEY, one of the LORD PALMERSTON, two of the CLARENDON, and one of the PITT'S HEAD. LORD DENMAN alone seems to have been selected to represent the legal profession. Among great military commanders, we have the MARQUIS OF GRANBY (represented by three examples), the LORD RAGLAN (by three), the LORD GOUGH (by one), the MARLBOROUGH'S HEAD (by three—one of which is mentioned in the *Chelmsford Chronicle* in 1764, while another at Maldon, not now existing, is mentioned in the same paper on March 2, 1787), and the *BLUCHER'S HEAD (by one at Romford). The KING OF PRUSSIA still figures as a sign at *Stratford. Prominent· Indian officers seem to be well represented. Thus we have a GENERAL HAVELOCK (very modern), a SIR COLIN CAMPBELL, and a SIR JOHN LAWRENCE. Sign-writers seem to have been unable to keep pace with the rapid promotion of these gentlemen. For instance, the first became Sir Henry Havelock so long ago as 1857; the second became Lord Clyde in the same year, and died in 1863; while the third was created Lord Lawrence in 1869, and died in 1879. Eminent naval commanders are commemorated by four examples of the LORD NELSON, one of the NELSON'S HEAD, and one of the LORD NAPIER. Sixty years ago, too, there was a *DUNCAN'S HEAD at Colchester. It was doubtless in honour of Admiral Duncan, who died in 1804. Larwood and Hotten do not notice this sign. The RODNEY at Little Baddow is a house well known to the worshippers of " St. Lubbock " and to other holiday-keepers in the neighbourhood of Chelmsford. It, of course, commemorates Admiral Lord Rodney, who died in 1792.

Mr. H. W. King writes :

"The taking of Porto Bello in 1739, and the popularity of Admiral Vernon at the time, caused many VERNON'S HEADS. One formerly existing at *Rochford is now demolished and has ceased to be. Either entirely new inns were thus named, or else old signs were abolished to make way for the portrait of the new favourite. Probably there were often similar changes for the sake of popularity."

One of the most notable signs in the county belonging to this class is the SIR WILFRID LAWSON at Woodford. It will be quite unnecessary to state that this is not an ordinary inn-sign. A Conservative politician would be more likely to deliver himself of an oration in praise of Mr. Gladstone and his virtues, than a publican to erect a sign to the honour of Sir Wilfrid Lawson. The house which exhibits this sign is a Coffee Tavern erected by an ardent abstainer and opened by Sir Wilfrid in May, 1883. The following amusing lines were penned by a member of the company present at the opening. They are, it is said, still to be seen in the house.

" All hops abandon, ye who enter here ;
    The wicked Wilfrid haunts this Watery Cavern ;
No wine, no whisky, nor even bitter beer,
    Flow through the channels of this Coffee Tavern.
The steaming coffee and the fragrant tea
    Are ready, where each eye can plainly see 'em ;
Tea-total, then, let each incomer be,
    And while ' Te-total' let him sing Te Deum."

On the map of the road between London and Harwich, given in Ogilby's *Itinerarium Angliæ*, published in 1675, a house—presumably an inn—called the MONK'S HEAD is shown on the east side of the road, exactly opposite New Hall Park. There can be no doubt that this sign represented, not the head of an ecclesiastic, but that of General Monk, the great promoter of the Restoration, although he had been created Duke of Albemarle some fifteen years before. After the Restoration, New Hall was purchased by, or for, General

Monk, and he lived there, as Morant says, "in very great splendour, to the diminution of his estates." He died in 1670, and was succeeded by his son. Forty years ago there was a FRIAR'S Inn in Fryer's Street, Chelmsford, but it has now disappeared. At Rayleigh there is a PAUL PRY (beer-house). At Widford a beer-house keeper has adopted as his sign that modern, though distinguished, Essex worthy, SIR EVELYN WOOD. Another at Waltham Abbey has selected the SULTAN. Others, at Saffron Walden and Waltham Abbey respectively, do honour to the OLD ENGLISH GENTLEMAN. Probably these latter have in their minds the hero of the song, rather than any gentleman in particular. At Theydon Garnon there is a MERRY FIDDLERS, which displays no less than three sign-boards. At Becontree Heath there is a beer-shop with the same sign. The landlord of the former states that, although he has endeavoured to unearth the meaning of his sign, he has hitherto failed. He adds, however, that, previous to his own occupation, the house had been in one family for many generations, and that for long it displayed a pictorial sign-board representing THREE FIDDLERS, but these have of late given place to the present sign. What particular three fiddlers are meant, is difficult to explain. The house bore merely its present name of the MERRY FIDDLERS in 1789. Larwood and Hotten do not mention the sign. At Abbots Roothing there is a COOPERS (beerhouse), a sign which is doubtless the same as that of the COOPERS' Arms. At Willingale Doe there is a FERRY MAN. Probably he has retired from business and settled there, as it is hard to discover any ferry at that place. About sixty-five years ago *BISHOP BLAYS, the patron saint of wool-combers, appeared as a sign at Colchester. It was a most appropriate sign in that town in the seventeenth century, when it was an important seat of the woollen trade. *NEPTUNE appears beside his "native element" at the Hythe, Colchester. Sixty years ago there was a *JOLLY SAILOR at Harwich, a *SAILOR'S RETURN at Grays, and a *MARINER at Colchester. These signs were all appropriate enough, being situated in maritime places, but the same cannot be said of the *THREE MARINERS which appeared at Chelmsford at the same period. Sixty years ago, too, there was to be seen at Colchester the curious sign of the *SAILOR AND BALL, which Larwood and Hotten do not mention. Probably it was not an impaled sign, but took its name from some game of ball played by sailors.

Numerous other signs are connected with Royalty. Thus we have two examples of the ALBERT, one of the ROYAL ALBERT, one of the ALBERT HOUSE, one of the KING OF PRUSSIA (formerly a very common sign), one of the QUEEN ADELAIDE (which is at least forty years old), one of the QUEEN ELIZABETH, four of the PRINCE ALFRED, one of the DUKE OF CAMBRIDGE, two of the DUKE OF EDINBURGH (neither of which existed twenty years ago), one of the CLARENCE (of course commemorating the Duke of Clarence, afterwards King William IV.), three of the DUKE OF YORK (probably commemorating the second son of George III., who died in 1827, though one or more of the earlier Dukes of York may also be intended), five of the ROYAL INN, one of the QUEEN, one of the QUEEN VICTORIA, ten of the VICTORIA, one of the ROYAL SOVEREIGN, one of the ROYAL ARMS, one of the ROYAL FOREST HOTEL, one ROYAL STEAMER, one ROYAL ESSEX ARMS, five of the ROYAL HOTEL, eighteen of the ROYAL OAK, one of the OLD ROYAL OAK, one of the KING'S OAK, four of the ROYAL STANDARD, three of the QUEEN'S ARMS, nineteen of the QUEEN'S HEAD, seventeen of the KING'S ARMS, forty-nine of the KING'S HEAD, one of the OLD KING'S HEAD, twelve of the PRINCE OF WALES, one of the PRINCESS OF WALES, one of the PRINCE ALBERT VICTOR, one of the PRINCESS ALICE, two of the PRINCESS ALEXANDRA, one of WILLIAM THE CONQUEROR (at Widdington), two of WILLIAM THE FOURTH, and two of KING WILLIAM THE FOURTH, one of which is placed at a "four-want-way" at Leaden Roothing, and forms a landmark well known to every one who rides to hounds or travels by road in "The Roothings." The KING WILLIAM and the KING WILLIAM IV. are both common beer-house signs, probably because the act authorizing the opening of these houses was passed in his reign. The beer-retailers of

the time, when casting about for a sign, naturally selected the
sovereign of their day. In the first form the sign occurs at
Bocking, Springfield, &c., and under the latter at Braintree,
Chigwell, and elsewhere. The PRINCE OF WALES, too, is a
very common beer-house sign, as also the VICTORIA, the
QUEEN VICTORIA, the QUEEN'S HEAD, and the QUEEN'S
ARMS. PRINCE ALFRED is commemorated on a beer-house
sign at Chigwell. At the same place is a BRITISH QUEEN
(beer-house), by which probably is intended Queen Boadicea,.
who received her last overthrow in the neighbourhood. The
PRINCE OF ORANGE still figures as a beer-house sign at
Chelmsford. The sign of PRINCE OF WALES' HEAD existed
at Harwich in 1764, as it is mentioned in a number of the
Chelmsford Chronicle for that year; and a ROYAL MORTAR
(whatever that might be) was to be seen at Colchester
twenty years ago. Messrs. Larwood and Hotten mention
the strange sign of the *THREE QUEENS, which was, until
lately, to be seen at Moulsham. They surmise that it was
suggested by the common sign of the THREE KINGS, of
which we have no example in Essex, unless the THREE
TRAVELLERS, which occurs near Romford, and is apparently
unique, be another form of it. The three kings represent
the three wise men or Magi from the East. A writer in
Notes and Queries (1st Series, vol. viii. p. 627) says that the
following rhyme was formerly appended to the sign of a
VICTORIA beer-shop at Coopersale :—

> " The Queen some day
> May pass this way
> And see our Tom and Jerry ; [1]
> Perhaps she'll stop
> And stand a drop
> To make her subjects merry."

On the other side of the sign-board were some different lines.
which the writer had forgotten.

The sign of the KING'S HEAD is by no means of modern
introduction. It occurs on the seventeenth century tokens
of Robert Adson of Colchester in 1668, of Thomas Bribrist of

[1] The use of the term " Tom and Jerry " has already been mentioned.
(p. 26).

Felstead (no date), and of Thomas Livermer of Wethersfield, and it is mentioned in advertisements in the *Chelmsford Chronicle* for March 10, 1787, as then occurring at Prittlewell and Stebbing. As the sign still exists at all these places, except Felstead and Wethersfield, it is at least probable that the same houses which were known by it in the seventeenth and eighteenth centuries are known by it now. The famous KING'S HEAD, opposite the church at Chigwell, so well described by Dickens in *Barnaby Rudge* under the name of the MAYPOLE, has been already spoken of (p. 113). It is a long, large, plastered building, with many gables, and projecting upper storeys—evidently dating from the era of the Stuarts or earlier. Arthur Young, in 1771, declares that " of all the cursed roads that ever disgraced this kingdom in the very ages of barbarism, none ever equalled that from Billericay to the KING'S HEAD at Tilbury." In 1678 a KING'S HEAD at Rickling formed a house of call for Poor Robin on his *Perambulation from Saffron Walden to London.* After recounting how he fared at the BLACK BULL at Newport, he says—

> "We having dined and joined a pint or two,
> Then forwards on my journey I did go ;
> And first came unto a town called Rickling,
> Where for to stay I made no stickling,
> But presently at the King's Head fell a tippling,
> Where of Compounding Dick [1] I there heard tell."

The KING'S HEAD on the Balkern Hill, Colchester, is an ancient and memorable inn, though the present house is not very old. At the time of the surrender of the town to Fairfax, in 1648, it was a general *rendezvous* of the noblemen and gentry of the Royalist party. Foxe, too, in his *Book of Martyrs* mentions that "at the KINGE'S HEAD in Colchester, and at other innes in the sayd towne, the afflicted Christians had set places appointed for themselves to meet at." Mr. H. W. King has kindly informed the author that the KING'S HEAD, now existing at Leigh, is not the same house as one which existed there under the same name in the

---

[1] A usurer.

eighteenth century. The latter is traceable (writes Mr. King) as a private house from 1671 to about 1720, being described in 1702 as a " messuage and shop." Between 1718 and 1723 it was rebuilt, as in the latter year it is spoken of as a new house, and is described as an inn with the sign of the QUEEN'S HEAD. In 1740 it is described as " the ANGEL, heretofore the QUEEN'S HEAD." In 1766 it is described as "the KING'S HEAD, heretofore the QUEEN'S HEAD, afterwards the ANGEL." It then became a private house, as it has ever since remained. It was probably soon after this, about 1766, that the present KING'S HEAD at Leigh assumed that name. These three changes, all within the short space of fifty years, or less, are very interesting. They seem to suggest that the house was first named the QUEEN'S HEAD in honour of Queen Anne; but that, when she died in 1714, the same sign (perhaps slightly altered) was made to do duty for some time as an ANGEL, and still later was changed to the KING'S HEAD, probably on the accession of one of the Georges. At Harold Wood there is a KING HAROLD, which is no doubt connected with the name of the place. At Nazing, which was one of the estates with which Harold endowed the neighbouring Abbey of Waltham, there has been for at least a century past a KING HAROLD'S HEAD.

The GEORGE, which occurs seventeen times in Essex, is another royal sign. In some instances it doubtless represents St. George, our patron saint, disconnected from his dragon; but, more probably, it has usually been set up—at least, of late—in honour of our Hanoverian kings. There is, however, abundant evidence that even as early as the very beginning of the seventeenth century, St. George, the Patron Saint of England, had already appeared on the sign-board without his usual antagonist the Dragon. Thus, " Blague, the merry host of the GEORGE at Waltham," figures prominently in *The Merry Divel of Edmonton*, published in 1617—a curious play, which Kirkman attributed to Shakespeare. The scene is partly laid in Waltham Forest. Poor Robin, too, in his *Perambulation* also mentions a GEORGE at Bishops Stortford in 1678. Mr. H. W. King also finds evidence in

ancient deeds that the GEORGE at Leigh was an inn as early
as 1680, but the house itself is probably somewhat earlier.
In 1777 it is described as "now and for some time past
known as the sign of the George." It had ceased to be an inn
by 1801, though then and long afterwards described as " a
messuage called the George," the words "known by the
sign of" being omitted. It was also a brewery. Mr. King
also finds evidence in other ancient deeds of the existence of
a GEORGE at Rayleigh in 1623, but whether an inn, shop, or
private house, does not appear. The *GEORGE at Epping
(perhaps identical with the GEORGE AND DRAGON which now
occurs there) is mentioned in the *Chelmsford Chronicle* in
1764 ; while the GEORGE at Halstead and the *GEORGE at
Witham (perhaps both identical with the well-known houses
now existing under the same name at each of those places)
are frequently referred to in advertisements in the same
paper for 1786, the latter as being then to let. A small
stone slab, let into the front of the GEORGE AND DRAGON Inn
at Wanstead, bears the following inscription :—

"*Restorat.* 1858. R. C.—In memory of yᵉ Cherrey Pey as cost ½ a
Guiney, yᵉ 17th of July, 1752.

> That day we had good cheer,
> I hope to so do many a year.—David Jersey."

The GEORGE AND DRAGON also occurs eight times elsewhere
in the county, as well as on several beer-house signs. At
Chelmsford there is an OLD GEORGE (beer-house). Mr. H.
W. King also finds mention in early deeds of a house known
as the GEORGE AND TANKARD at Shopland in 1579. It is not
stated that it was an inn, but from the sign there can be very
little doubt that it was. The appearance of an apparently
impaled sign at so early a date is certainly very remarkable.
Larwood and Hotten do not notice this device.

Various military signs occur at places where there are
barracks. For instance, there are at Colchester houses with
such signs as the BUGLE HORN, the ARTILLERY-MAN, the
RIFLEMAN, the DRAGOON, the *FENCERS (a sign which is at
least forty years old, though it is not mentioned by Larwood

and Hotten), an ORDNANCE ARMS, and a ROYAL ARTILLERY;
whilst at Great Warley there is a HORSE ARTILLERY and a SOLDIER'S HOTEL, which seems to have been the SOLDIER'S HOPE forty years ago. At Waltham Abbey there is a VOLUNTEER; there are RIFLEMEN at Colchester and Black Notley (beerhouse); at Kelvedon Hatch there is a GUARDSMAN, at Rettendon a LIFE GUARDS, and at Leyton a GRENADIER. The figure of a Grenadier, here reproduced, is taken from the *Gentleman's Magazine* for December, 1845 (p. 591), to which it was contributed by the late Mr. J. A. Repton, F.S.A., formerly of Springfield. A SOLDIER is represented on three different farthing tokens issued by John Allen of Braintree, one of which bears the date 1657. All bear his initials, but one has the inscription, "Turne a penny," in the place of the name of the issuer.

GRENADIER.

On these tokens the orthography is decidedly peculiar. Thus,

10

Braintree is twice spelled "Brantre" and once "Brantry," while Essex is twice spelled "Esex" and once "Esaxes."

Among the more miscellaneous of Human Signs we meet with a CROWN'S INN at Ongar, a FORESTER at Coggeshall, a FORESTER'S INN at Plaistow, an ANCIENT FORESTERS at Hatfield Broad Oak (all, of course, connected with the "ancient order"), three FREEMASONS' TAVERNS, several FREEMASONS' ARMS, a MERRY FIDDLERS at Theydon Garnon, eight examples of the CRICKETERS (against five in 1862), two of the CRICKETERS' ARMS, a JOLLY CRICKETERS, a JOLLY FISHERMAN, a JOLLY SAILOR, a SAILOR'S RETURN, two WELCOME SAILORS, an OLD WELCOME SAILOR, a THREE TRAVELLERS (perhaps representing the three wise men from the East), and a MINERVA at Southend, which, as Mr. H. W. King has ascertained, was recently christened by its owner after a barge of the same name that he possessed. At Chigwell there has been for at least a century past a house with the sign of the THREE JOLLY WHEELERS (whatever they might be). There are TRAVELLERS' FRIENDS at Moulsham and Woodford Wells (the former being at least forty years old), as well as a beer-house of the same name at Epping; TRAVELLERS' RESTS at Forest Gate and Wethersfield (the latter being a beer-house); BRITANNIAS at Canning Town, Barking, Southend, and Hornchurch (beer-house); and Two BREWERS at *Stratford, Springfield, High Ongar, and Chigwell (beer-house). This is a sign once common, but now becoming rare. They were usually represented carrying a barrel of beer between them, slung on a pole. There are WOODMEN at Halstead, Elmdon, Waltham Abbey, Stanford Rivers, Thundersley, Romford, &c., all but the first two being beer-houses. The THREE MARINERS is an odd sign which occurs at Colchester and at Moulsham (Chelmsford). At the latter place it seems to have existed for at least a century, being referred to in the *Chelmsford Chronicle* for January 27, 1786. In the garden of the ADAM AND EVE at West Ham (p. 37) stands the remains of an old stone arch, now almost the only remaining portion of the ancient abbey of Stratford Langthorn. In the kitchen are (or were lately) a coffin, a seal, some coins, and some urns dug up in an adjoining field towards the end of last century. The ESSEX HEAD, in Essex Street, Strand, London, W.C., probably commemorates the Earl of Essex, who was a favourite of Queen Elizabeth, rather than the county of that name. It clearly either takes its name from, or gives its name to, the street in which it stands. The inn was established in the last century. On the Forest, near High Beech, is a beer-shop known as the DICK TURPIN'S CAVE. It clearly takes its name from a hole in the ground not far distant, commonly spoken of as "Dick Turpin's Cave." The "cave" (if such it ever was) is now thickly overgrown with trees and brushwood. It is well known that Messrs. Dick Turpin and Co. especially haunted the neighbourhood of Epping and Hainault Forests, and until the end of last century it was not considered safe to traverse the roads thereabouts unless well armed. It may very well be, therefore, that the famous highwayman did, at some time or other, use this hole as a place of refuge.

The HERCULES at Newport (the only example in Essex of this rather uncommon sign) has already been mentioned (p. 65), also the tradition that the BULL, which stood opposite to it, was by it compelled to close its doors. With regard to this inn Mr. C. K. Probert of Newport sends an interesting note. He says:

"The HERCULES stands next to the old Vicarage. Now we know it was a common custom among village clergymen to take their pipe and pot at the village inn, as mentioned in the old song, which says:

'At the sign of the Horse,
Old Spintext, of course,
Each night takes his pipe and his pot,
O'er a Jorum of "nappy,"
Contented and happy,
There sits this canonical sot,' &c., &c.

Further, it is my belief that the HERCULES was started in opposition to the BULL, our Pastor (being the most learned individual in the place at the period) probably suggesting the classical name, in reference to the seventh labour of Hercules—the slaying of the Cretan Bull."

Forty years ago there existed at Colchester a MALTSTER'S INN, a MARINER'S INN, and a NEPTUNE; at Stratford a CHINAMAN, and at Tendring a CROWN AND BLACKSMITH, the latter being, perhaps, an impaled sign signifying that the landlord of the CROWN was also a blacksmith.

It will be most convenient to treat of the sign of the ANGEL, which occurs eleven times in Essex, among Human Signs, although an angel is commonly accounted to be something more than human. An ANGEL occurs on the seventeenth-century tokens of "Francis Aleyn at the Angell in Brentwood," of "Georg Silke at the Angell in Rvmford," of Francis Dilke, also of Rumford, of William Hartley of Colchester, and of George Taylor of Ilford in 1665. As the sign still exists at the two last-named places, the probabilities are that the two houses bearing it are identical with those from which the tokens were issued a couple of centuries ago. The ANGEL at Ilford was formerly a posting-house of great importance; but, like its neighbour, the RED LION, and all the other once-busy inns on this great highway from London into the Eastern counties, it is now sadly decayed from its old importance, though still a house of high standing. Its massive sign-post and ornamental sign-iron date from at least a century ago. Probably it was at this house that, on August 18, 1662, Pepys, "while dinner was getting ready, practised measuring of the tables and other things, till [as he says] I did understand measure of timber and board very well." This he did that he might know how to detect fraud on the part of those who bought timber for the navy. Taylor (see p. 28) in 1636 mentions ANGELS at Romford and Brentwood, which do not now exist. The *ANGEL in the High Street at Colchester is, perhaps, the modern representative of the ANGEL mentioned in one of the Corporation records (see p. 62) as being an "auncyent inne" in 1603. There are beer-houses with the same sign at Braintree, Bocking, and elsewhere. In the Corporation records of Saffron Walden for the year 1645 it appears that the sum of 6s. 2d. was expended upon "a pottle of sack, 3 qts. of claret and white wine burnt, for the committee, when they sat at the ANGEL." This is probably the same house which continued to exist in Gould Street up to about fifty years ago, when it was kept by one Butterfield, who was also a barber, and who displayed the following rhyme upon his sign-board :

> "Rove not from pole to pole, but call in here,
> Where nought exceeds the shaving, but the beer."

The pole referred to is, of course, the barber's pole. The couplet was, however, not original. The ANGEL, which still continues to exist at Kelvedon, is referred to in an advertise-ment in the *Chelmsford Chronicle* for December 29, 1786. It is also stated in the Bufton MSS.[1] that on the 20th of October, 1692, King William III. "stayed and dined at the ANGELL," at Kelvedon. Doubtless he was on his way to Holland, *viâ* Harwich. Larwood and Hotten say (p. 266) that this sign " was derived from the Salutation ; for, that it originally represented the Angel appearing to the Holy Virgin at the Salutation or Annunciation, is evident from the fact that, even as late as the seventeenth century, on nearly all the trades-tokens of houses with this sign, the Angel is represented with a scroll in his hands ; and this scroll we know, from the evidence of paintings and prints, to contain the words addressed by the Angel to the Holy Virgin : '*Ave Maria, gratia plena, Dominus tecum.*' Probably at the Refor-mation it was considered too Catholic a sign, and so the Holy Virgin was left out, and the Angel only retained." The supporters of the arms of Richard II. were also two angels, blowing trumpets. The ANGEL AND HARP at Church End, Dunmow, is a strange sign which does not appear to be noticed by the authors so often quoted. Prob-ably it is a modern, though by no means inappropriate, impalement, as it appears in the list of sixty years ago simply as the *HARP.

The sign of the BLACK BOY occurs seven times in the county, namely, at Chelmsford, Wrabness, Bocking, Weeley, *Coggeshall, Wivenhoe, and Great Bromley. At the latter place it seems to have existed since 1786, as a sale is adver-tised to take place at the BLACK BOY in Great Bromley, in the *Chelmsford Chronicle* for March 3rd in that year. There

---

[1] *Trans. Essex Arch. Soc.*, vol. i. p. 125.

is also a beer-house of this name at Danbury, and the large brick house in the High Street at Epping, lately occupied by that eminent naturalist, Henry Doubleday, was an inn with this sign before the Doubleday family acquired it about 1770. The BLACK BOY now existing at Chelmsford is not the same house that went under that name during the last and previous centuries, though standing on the same site. The old inn ranked as a coaching-inn of the first importance. It was pulled down in 1857, having been fairly run off the road by the opening of the railway in 1843. Two wooden bosses, taken from the ceiling of one of the rooms, and now to be seen in the Chelmsford Museum, are carved, respectively, with the Blue Boar of the De Veres (to which family the house probably once belonged), and the red and white rose combined. Mr. John Adey Repton, F.S.A., formerly of Springfield, writing to the *Gentleman's Magazine* in May, 1840, sends sketches of these two bosses, which were duly inserted. He says :

"There is a tradition that Richard III. was hunting in the forest, and being missed by his courtiers was afterwards found at this house. . . . The beam is massive, being not less than 16 inches wide. The room, although only 9½ feet high, was originally a hall 28½ feet long, but subsequently reduced to 18½ feet by a partition, leaving a passage to the inn. Yet this partition, from the style and character of the panels, appears to have been added so early as the reign of Henry VIII. The doors to the buttery-hatch, &c., may still be traced on the wall of the passage."

Writing again to the same Magazine in December, 1845, Mr. Repton says :

"I send you a sketch of a Chambermaid. The figure is now at the White Hart, Chelmsford, having been recently removed thither from the Black Boy. It was formerly the custom in ancient family mansions to introduce a painting which represents a housemaid holding a broom in her hands, which was cut out of a board, and generally placed in a passage or at the top of the stairs. The earliest specimens I have seen are of the date of Charles I., or the early part of Charles II. . . . The enclosed specimen is of a later period, having the Fontaine head-dress which prevailed about the time of William III. or Queen Anne. . . . Sometimes the figure of a soldier, like a sentry, was exhibited in like manner. . . . Such a figure is on the staircase of the Bull at Dartford. Another, of which I send you a sketch [see p. 129], is at the Black Boy in Chelmsford."

Mr. Chancellor of Chelmsford writes that—

"In 1424 [when Chelmsford Church was largely built] John De Vere, 12th Earl of Oxford, was at the head of that family, having succeeded to the title in 1415. From his known adherence to the House of Lancaster, he may be presumed to have been a person of some importance, and as a consequence in constant communication with the Court. Undoubtedly, therefore, he would journey to and from Hedingham Castle, his baronial seat, to London, many times in the course of the year ; and as it would appear that the old hostelry, known as the Black Boy, in this town, belonged to the De Vere family, it is a very fair presumption that Chelmsford was not only a halting-place for the Earl and his retainers upon the occasion of their journeys, but probably used as an occasional residence ; and as he lived in almost royal state, his comings to and fro would be a matter of as much importance to the then townsfolk as a visit of the sovereign in the present day. . . . We can readily believe that so powerful and wealthy a man would be the first applied to for aid. That he did assist, is proved by the fact of his shield, charged with the mullet, being carved in the spandrel of the west door of the tower ; and his crest, the boar, being introduced in the apex of the arch of the same door ; this latter corresponds with the carved boar which formed part of the ceiling of an apartment in the old Black Boy [see p. 71]. For five centuries did this mighty family rule it most royally over many parts of the country, their riches being immense, and their power and influence being second only to the sovereign ; and yet now a cubic foot of stone in our parish church, and a cubic foot of oak deposited in our museum, are all that remain in this town to remind us of the De Veres."

A good view of this famous old inn is given in Ryland's view of Chelmsford High Street, engraved in 1762, and reproduced as the frontispiece of this volume. From it, in all probability, our six other Essex Black Boys have taken their name, as the sign is unusually common in the county. It stood at the corner of Springfield Lane and the High Street. The *Ipswich Express*, in speaking of the closing of this ancient house, which, as it remarked, had been "for centuries one of the oldest inns on the road," remarked as follows :—

"There are not only pleasant recollections of 'slippered ease,' but historical associations, connected with the old Inn. Here royal heads have rested, and warriors have halted as they hurried off to draw the sword on fields of military renown. Within its rooms, martyrs have passed the last night of life, in the fiery days of religious persecution, on their way to the fatal stake. In the old war, its roof often resounded with the mad jollity of prizemen and privateers, who had just brought their rich booty into Harwich, and, as they posted off to London, had halted at the well-known hostelry to make merry with their gains. A quarter of a century ago, between forty and fifty stage-coaches passed its door daily, most of which pulled up, if they did not pause, to allow the travellers to partake of the provision made for them ; while numberless pairs of post-horses stood saddled in its capacious stables."

Dickens mentions this house in *Pickwick Papers* (1st Edition, p. 161), when Mr. Weller, Senior, relates how he transported Messrs. Job Trotter and Charles Fitz-Marshall from "the Black Boy at Chelmsford . . . right through to Ipswich." Mr. Chancellor has ascertained that, in a deed dated 1642, this inn is described as "heretofore known by the name or sign of the CROWN or NEW INN, or the KING'S ARMS, and later as the BLACK BOY." That it was the BLACK BOY in 1636 is certain, for Taylor, "the Water Poet," in his *Catalogue of Tavernes*, mentions it as one of the chief inns in the town at that time. In 1660, the Rev. R. E. Bartlett finds it recorded in the Chelmsford registers that "Andrew Speller, a dumb man, who lived at the Black Boy in Chelmsford, was buried the 2 day of August." It has probably retained the same sign ever since. This frequent change at so early a date is very interesting. It seems to indicate (as Mr. Chancellor suggests) that, on the house passing out of the hands of the De Veres, it became an inn, and that, although it may have displayed the sign of the CROWN (see p. 166), it was commonly known as the NEW INN. Afterwards, for some reason, it came to be styled the KING'S ARMS, and still later the BLACK BOY, though why, it is not apparent. At the time of his demise, this "Old Boy" (as he may be familiarly styled) was, therefore, at least 250 years old. It might be thought strange that having existed so long, and having begat the seven sons already mentioned, he never grew into a "Black Man," but died as he had so long lived, a "Black Boy"! A BLACK BOY formerly existed in Saffron Walden, as shown by the following entries in the Corporation records:—"March 27th, 1682, 'Spent at the Black Boy 12 pence,'" and a little later 4s. 6d. was "spent at the Black Boy with the Chamberlains when we assessed the fines on the Quakers." In the Waltham Abbey parish register is the following entry:—"Judith Sutton, from ye Blacks, Bur. May 26, 1740." This was probably the BLACK

Boy Inn that formerly stood in Town-mead Lane. The BLACK BOY is a sign of venerable antiquity. From the first it has been largely used as a tobacconist's sign. The crest of the Tobacco-pipe Makers' Company, incorporated in 1663, was a demi-Moor, while the supporters were *two young Moors proper, wreathed about the loins with tobacco leaves vert.* A black Saracen's head, too, was the badge of Lord Cobham in the time of Edward IV., and also of Sir John Harlwyn.

Essex contains at the present time no less than twenty-seven houses showing the sign of the GREEN MAN. The GREEN MAN at Leyton is mentioned in the ·*Trials of Swan and Jeffries* in 1752, while the GREEN MAN at Leytonstone is mentioned by Daniel Defoe in his *Tour through Great Britain,* first published in 1724, and is also marked on Roque's ·*Map of Ten Miles round London,* published in 1741. It is recorded in the *Gentleman's Magazine* (vol. xxiii. p. 148) that Charles, Earl of Tankerville, died of an apoplectic fit at the GREEN MAN on Epping Forest on the 14th of March, 1753, as he was travelling to London. Old maps of the latter half of last century show quite a number of GREEN MEN round Epping and Hainault Forests, showing the connection even then existing in the minds of men between the sign-board GREEN MEN and foresters. In Mr. Creed's list of signs round Epping in 1789, GREEN MEN are named at the following places: Epping, Waltham Abbey, Moreton, Stanford Rivers, Magdalen Laver, Harlow, and Roydon. Evidently this sign was very common a century ago. Although this device has a two-fold origin, it is rather difficult to account for its great prevalence in the present day. Originally, no doubt, the sign represented the green-clad morris-dancers that played an important part in the shows and pageants of mediæval times; but, when these went out of date and were forgotten by the common people, the sign was made to represent a forester in his coat of green. As early as the seventeenth century the sign had come to be connected with that celebrated forester, Robin Hood, as is shown by the designs on many of the tokens, which represent the outlaw accompanied by his friend

Little John. At Elsenham and at High Beech the sign now takes the name of the ROBIN HOOD, while ROBIN HOOD AND LITTLE JOHN occur in combination at Brentwood, although in an advertisement in the *Chelmsford Chronicle* for January 20, 1786, the house is spoken of simply as the ROBIN HOOD. At High Beech, as is often the case, the following couplet is appended to the sign :—

> "If Robin Hood be not at home,
> Step in and ask for Little John."

Mrs. F. B. Palliser says,[1] " Queen Anne bore, as one of the supporters of her arms, one of the savage men, wreathed with ivy and bearing clubs, of Denmark, since designated and adopted for an inn-sign as the GREEN MAN." This, however, is probably not the only origin of the sign. At the present day the sign is generally represented on Essex sign-boards by a gamekeeper in a green velveteen coat. At Grays there is a GREEN MAN AND BELL (beer-house), which is doubtless an impaled sign.

A beer-shop at Great Chesterford displays a pictorial sign —evidently of some age—representing, apparently, the MAN AND PLOUGH. A rustic in a green smock-frock stands at the handle of his plough, politely touching his hat to passers-by.

At Chelmsford and Dunmow the principal inn in each of the two towns has for its sign the SARACEN'S HEAD. The former is mentioned in the *Chelmsford Chronicle* for January 6, 1786. It is also many times named in the *Trials of Swan and Jeffries* in 1752, on account of a robbery having been committed there. It also finds mention in Mr. Joseph Strutt's Essex and Herts romance, entitled *Queenhoo Hall*, published in 1808. The hero of the tale says (ii. p. 179) that "on my arrival at Chelmsford, I went to one of the principal inns, distinguished by the sign of the Saracen, or Man Quintain, where I took some small refreshment." Other examples, making five in all, occur at Danbury, Braintree, and Thaxted. Though not described by Boyne,

[1] *Historic Devices, Badges,* &c., p. 386.

tokens, bearing a representation of a Saracen's head, and issued by John Havers at the house of that name in Thaxted, are still extant, showing the house and its sign to be of considerable antiquity. Mr. Joseph Clarke, F.S.A., of Saffron Walden can recollect that, many years ago, the sign-board bore the representation of a man's head with a very ferocious countenance, but the sign-board is not now pictorial. The sign owes its origin (largely, at least) to the Crusades. It was formerly much more common than now.

The MAID'S HEAD at Thorpe-le-Soken is, in all probability, not a sign put up by some enamoured publican. As a general rule the sign, wherever it appears, has been derived from the arms of the Mercers' Company, already given (p. 33). Sir William Parr, K.G., and also his grand-daughter, Queen Catherine Parr, both bore the same device as a badge. But in the case of the example at Thorpe there can be little doubt that the sign is a really ancient one, and that it represents the crest of the D'Arcy family, Barons of Chiche,[1] to whom, in 1551, Edward VI. granted the manor of Thorpe and neighbouring lands, which long afterwards remained in the family. The same sign often occurs elsewhere as the MAIDEN HEAD. There was apparently a house of this name (not necessarily an inn) at Chelmsford in the seventeenth century, as the Rev. R. E. Bartlett finds the following entry in the parish registers :—" 1620, Matthew Prentys of Chelmsford, husbandman and householder at the Maidenhead in Chelmsford, was buried the xiiii. of May, being Sunday." The VILLAGE MAID, which occurs at Bradfield, is a very modern sign, and is not mentioned by Larwood and Hotten. Probably the landlord set it up in honour of some damsel of his acquaintance.

The MERMAID, though only a semi-human sign, is most conveniently noticed here. There is no example of it now existing in the county, though it occurs on the farthing token of Michael Arnold of Colchester. As a sign it used formerly to be not uncommon.

[1] A demi-woman, hair flowing proper, vested gules holding in the dexter hand three roses, slipped and leaved vert.

The *Silent Woman is the name of a public-house, with a truly pictorial sign, at Widford. The signs of the Good Woman and the Quiet Woman, which occur occasionally in other counties, are identical with this, and, all alike, constitute a piece of unwarrantable slander on the fair sex, being intended to convey the idea that a woman can only be silenced by being deprived of her head. Larwood and Hotten say (p. 455):

> "There is a very curious example of this sign at Widford, near Chelmsford, representing on one side a half-length portrait of Henry VIII., on the reverse, a woman without a head, dressed in the costume of the latter half of the last century, with the inscription *Forte Bonne*. The addition of the portrait of Henry VIII. has led to the popular belief that the headless woman is meant for Anne Boleyn, though probably it is simply a combination of the King's Head and Good Woman."

THE SILENT WOMAN AT WIDFORD.

The inscription on the sign-board is, presumably, intended to be the French for "Very Good," but it is spelled "*Fort Bon,*" and it has been "*Fort Bone.*"

A writer in *Once a Week* (N. S., ii. p. 487) says:

> "The Essex tradition is that St. Osyth, when the convent was attacked by the Danes [A.D. 635], fled down the park to a thicket, since called 'Nun's Wood,' where she was overtaken, and her head cut off; and that on the spot where the head fell, a spring of water burst forth, which flows to this day. Another local tradition asserts that on one night in each year St. Osyth revisits the scene of her former abode, walking with her head under her arm. It is this legend which probably gave rise to the sign of the 'Good Woman,' at Widford, near Chelmsford,—of whom, by the way, I may remark that she is currently said to be the only good woman in Essex."

Larwood and Hotten say that the sign was largely used by oilmen, which makes it very probable that the device has some reference to the " heedless virgins " who had no oil in their lamps when the bridegroom came—*heed* and *head* having formerly been pronounced alike, according to those authors. The sign is not uncommon on the Continent also.

A writer in *Notes and Queries* (Fifth Series, vol. iv. p. 337) very ingeniously explains the origin of this sign. He says :

" In the days of old it was *la bone fame*, with a meaning the same as that of *la bonne renommée* in later times. According to Virgil, Fame walks on the earth while her head is concealed in the clouds—

' Ingrediturque solo, et caput inter nubila condit.'

Consequently *la bone fame* was represented by a headless woman—at times, no doubt, very roughly drawn. By degrees the word *fame* dropped out of the French language, and then people read *la bonne femme*, correcting what they deemed an orthographical error. But [then arose the question] why should the ' good woman ' have no head ? The explanation was, of course, suggested by some hen-pecked cynic at the wineshop."

On the high road between Braintree and Chelmsford, and in the parish of Great Leighs, stands an inn with the strange sign of the ST. ANN'S CASTLE. On the map of the road between Chelmsford and Bury, given in Ogilby's *Itinerarium Angliæ*, published in 1675, the words " St. Ann's " appear against a house beside the high road at Leighs and on the site of the present inn. It appears from this that the word " Castle " is a modern addition to the name, perhaps connected with the adjacent ruins of Leighs Priory. The house is, however, marked as the ST. ANN'S CASTLE on Greenwood's map of Essex, published as long ago as 1824. In White's *Gazetteer of Essex* it is stated that there formerly stood upon the spot a hermitage, known as St. Ann's, "where pilgrims rested on their way to and from the shrine of St. Thomas à Becket. At the Dissolution, in 1571, it was given to Thos. Jennings, and its site is now occupied by an inn, called the St. Ann's Castle, and said to be the oldest licensed public-house in England." Morant says of it in 1768, " 'Tis now converted into an ale-house." Probably it had become an inn much earlier, for Taylor, in 1636, mentions one Will. Chandler as being a keeper of "innes at Plashie and St. Annes."

According to G. W. Johnson's *History of Great Totham*, it is stated that a hill at that place "seems to have been dedicated to the Virgin Mary, for at its base is a small public-house known now [1831], and as far back as memory can go, as the VIRGIN'S TAVERN." The sign is not now in existence.

In speaking of the LAME DOG, which does not occur as a sign in this county, Larwood and Hotten say that it is sometimes accompanied by the following couplet :

" Stop, my friends, and stay awhile
To help the lame dog over the style."

They continue (p. 450) : "Sometimes, as at Bulmer, Essex, we see a somewhat similar idea expressed by a MAN STRUG-GLING through a globe—head and arms protruding on one side, his legs on the other—with the inscription, ' Help me through this world.' " This sign is not now to be seen at Bulmer.

A HAND occurs on the halfpenny token issued by Law-rence Brown, junior, of Wickham, in 1669; a HAND AND GLOVE on that of Henry Cordall of Chelmsford in 1658; a HAND AND PEN on that of Samuel Cox of Coggeshall ; and a HAND AND BALL on that of " D. G." issued at " The Hand and Bowle in Barking " in 1650. In 1675, a house of some kind displayed the sign of the CROSS AND HAND at Marks Tey (see p. 163). Although the hand does not now appear, either singly or in combination, on any Essex sign-board, it is not uncommon in other counties. Its use is attributable to the fact that early sign-painters often repre-sented it issuing out of a cloud to perform some action or support some object. This brings to a close the list of human signs now occurring in the county of Essex.

CHAPTER VIII.

HE small class which will next receive notice contains what may be called "Nautical Signs." Essex supports quite a considerable fleet of ships upon its sign-boards. These are of widely different builds, and are very variously rigged. Most of them are, of course, situated near the coast; but others are, strange to say, far inland. The author would be guilty of great impropriety did he not speak first of NOAH'S ARK—the greatest feat of early ship-building on record. As a sign, it was to be seen at Kelvedon twenty years ago, but is now non-existent. *An ark or, on the top a dove argent, holding in the beak an olive-branch vert,* forms the crest of the Shipwrights' Company, incorporated in 1605. As already stated, no less than twenty-two SHIPS are to be found in different parts of the county. ·The surmise that some of these are intended to represent *sheep* has been elsewhere advanced (p. 23). Mr. King finds evidence in ancient deeds of no less than three different houses at Leigh which have formerly borne the sign of the SHIP. The existing example was probably converted into an inn about the end of last century. It was a private house in the middle of the century. Another inn is first spoken of as the Ship in 1728. In 1732, it was "known by the sign of the Ship," but before 1756, when it was spoken of as "formerly known by the sign of the Ship," it had ceased to be an inn. The third and probably the earliest house of this name was a private residence in 1756, having formerly been called the SHIP. A SHIP is depicted on the

tokens of "William Martin at the Key [? Quay] in Barking,"
and of "Thomas Pollard at the [Ship] in Plaistowe," 1668,
and the SHIP at *Colchester is several times mentioned in
the advertisements appearing in the various numbers of the
Chelmsford Chronicle issued during February, 1786. The first
and last are, perhaps, identical with the houses of the same
name still existing at those places. In addition to the foregoing we have five OLD SHIPS. If Mr. Plimsoll were informed of this fact it would probably cause him some alarm;
but he would be reassured on learning that, with one exception, all are some distance inland. They are situated
respectively at West Thurrock, Debden, Chelmsford, Aveley,
and Rochford. The *OLD SHIP at the last-named place
must be in very unseaworthy condition, for it was described
as old in an advertisement in the Chelmsford Chronicle for
January 27, 1786. There is also a *NEW SHIP at Rochford—doubtless a house started in opposition to the OLD
SHIP at the same place. The sign of the *SHIP AND ANCHOR,
which occurs at Maldon, is a combination the meaning of
which will be at once apparent. The SHIP AND SHOVEL at
Rippleside, Barking, is at least forty years old. It is probably in some way connected with Sir Cloudesley Shovel, as
there is a portrait of that gentleman in the inn. The sign
also occurs elsewhere, namely, in Steel Yard, St. Thomas'
Street, London, S.E. An old newspaper cutting says a
house known as the SHIP AND SHOVEL "is situated near to
Dagenham Beach, in Essex, eleven miles from London,
where Parish and Hadbrook fought a hard battle of 41 rounds,
on the 13th of March, 1820, which terminated in favour
of Parish in thirty-eight minutes. The SHIP AND SHOVEL
was the house of call for that day." There is a LOBSTER
SMACK at Canvey Island, a FISHING SMACK at Barking, an
OYSTER SMACK at Burnham, and a SMACK at Leigh, concerning which Mr. H. W. King writes, that it was no doubt so
named when the oyster-fishery flourished there in the last
century. There is not now a smack belonging to the port.
The house itself was for centuries a private residence of
persons of good account. The sign of the PETER BOAT,

which also occurs at Leigh, is apparently unique. A peter-boat was a sort of fishing-vessel, sharp both stem and stern, and half-decked, with a spritsail, instead of a mainsail and boom. Mr. King states that the inn derives its name from the fact that " all the fishing-boats at Leigh were formerly peter-boats. But, out of a fleet of 120 or more fishing-boats here now, only one peter-boat, I am told, remains, and that I have not seen. The house itself, of the descent of which I have a complete record since 1645, is built of timber and is of the middle of the seventeenth century or earlier. The present owners have held it since 1662, the landlord who now keeps the inn being about the sixth in direct descent. It is first mentioned as known by the sign of the Peter-boat in 1757. The then owner had come into pos-session in 1739, and had so named the house between those years." At Vange there is a BARGE, at North Woolwich an OLD BARGE HOUSE, at Forest Gate a STEAMSHIP, and at Chelmsford a ROYAL STEAMER (probably an impaled sign). The Barge here mentioned was formerly the MAN WITH SEVEN WIVES, as Mr. King can recollect. At the time it belonged to a man named *Wife*. Presumably his family numbered seven individuals. There is also a beer-house of the same name at Rettendon, up to which place the river Crouch is navigable for barges. The PACKET occurs at *Harwich and *Manningtree. Sixty years ago there was another example at *Colchester. The sign of the FERRY-BOAT occurs at Walthamstow, North Fambridge, and Canew-don. Another house of the same name has recently dis-appeared from the county, as also a FERRY HOUSE. Sixty years ago the sign of the WHERRY (not noticed by Larwood and Hotten) occurred at *Mistley. The sign of the HOY still occurs at Tollesbury and at South Benfleet. Mr. King remarks that one would naturally expect to find this sign at the latter place, " as a long succession of hoymen carried on a lucrative business there. The HOY is now pictorially represented on the sign-board by a barge, though the house is still called the HOY; and a trade in hay, straw, and corn is still carried on in two or three barges." The sign is not

referred to in the *History of Sign-boards*. The following
epitaph upon a Hoyman appears in the churchyard at South
Benfleet. Though not a very scholarly production, it is said
to be the work of a former rector of the parish.

> "James Mathews, Ob. July 14, 1728.
> Sixty-three years our Hoyman sailed merrily round,
> Forty-four lived parishioner where he's aground,
> Five wives bare him thirty-three children—enough :
> Land another as honest before he gets half."

A hoy was a one-masted, sloop-rigged coasting vessel,
formerly much used. It is extremely difficult to suggest
any likely origin for the sign of the PLOUGH AND SAIL, which
occurs no less than four times in the county, namely, at
Tollesbury, East Hanningfield, Paglesham, and Maldon.
Larwood and Hotten do not allude to it. The two first are
each at least forty years old. At first one might suppose it
a meaningless impalement of two distinct signs, the PLOUGH
and the SAIL, but it does not appear that the latter figures
as a sign, either singly or in combination with any other
article except a plough, in any part of England. Moreover,
it is hardly likely that the two signs would appear impaled
four times in Essex, while the combination is (with one
exception) unknown in all other counties of England. An
examination of the lists of signs in thirty of the principal
counties of England will show that it does not occur in any
of them, with the exception of the adjoining county of Suffolk,
wherein the sign occurs twice. It appears probable, therefore, that the sign has some local significance, though it is
difficult to say exactly what. Several gentlemen have offered
suggestions as to its origin. It has been thought to be a
corruption of the " Plow and Flail " (and therefore doubly
agricultural), or a representation of the old toast of " Agricul-
ture and Commerce " (represented by a plough and a ship),
but the most likely suggestion seems to be one put forward
by the Rev. H. L. Elliot, who thinks it is intended as an
appeal for the custom of thirsty souls working both on land
and sea. All our Essex examples, except that at Hanningfield, are upon the coast. The same gentleman suggests that

the sign may be a corruption of the " Plough-tail " or handle, which Edwards, in his *Words, Facts, and Phrases,* says is probably derived from the Anglo-Saxon *stail,* a handle. The word is still in use, meaning a handle, in Warwickshire and other parts of the country. An appeal to the readers of *Notes and Queries* has so far thrown no light on the meaning of this sign. Forty years ago there was a SHIP AND EXCISE OFFICE at Waltham Abbey and a PRIVATEER at Harwich. At Wivenhoe there is a SHIP AT LAUNCH. Forty years ago it was known as the SHIP LAUNCH. This large fleet of sign-board ships is, however, supplied with only eighteen ANCHORS; and, as some of these may represent the symbol of Hope, the supply must be regarded as very inadequate. One of them, belonging to Barking, is described as a BLUE ANCHOR. Another of the same description used formerly to exist on Canvey Island, but it appears to have been lost in some storm during the last forty years ; while another at Mersey, which is mentioned in the Rev. Baring-Gould's *Mehalah,* has also disappeared, unless it be identical with the ANCHOR still existing at that place. The ANCHOR at Canewdon seems to have existed there since at least 1787, as it is mentioned in an advertisement in the *Chelmsford Chronicle* for the 5th of January in that year. At Grays there is an ANCHOR AND HOPE. The CROWN AND ANCHOR, the emblem of the Royal Navy, occurs at Aveley and Braintree ; and the SUN AND ANCHOR, which is probably nothing but an impaled sign, occurs at Steeple. A token is extant bearing an ANCHOR, the initials "R. S. I.," and the inscription, " At the Anker, in Lee [Leigh], 1664." Mr. H. W. King writes :[1] " This is undoubtedly the token of Robert Sayer and Joan his wife, shopkeepers, at this precise date. The ANCHOR was their shop sign. There was no inn of that name. Joan Sayer survived her husband and died in 1689." Most of our ANCHORS are situated upon the sea coast, but there are not a few inland— at Ingatestone, Chelmsford, Abbots Roothing, &c. In 1789 there was one at Chipping Ongar.

[1] *Trans. Essex Arch. Soc.,* N. S., vol. ii. part iv. p. 400.

CHAPTER IX.

ASTRONOMICAL SIGNS.

STRONOMICAL signs fall naturally into another small class, which will be treated of next. In Essex we have six examples of the sign of the HALF MOON, which may represent either crescents taken from some one's arms or else the emblem of temporal power. The HALF MOON at *Chelmsford, a small, though ancient, house, possesses a quaint and truly pictorial sign-board. At 94, Great Suffolk Street, London, S.E., there has been for three-quarters of a century, at least, a house with the most extraordinary sign of the MOONRAKERS. It is all but impossible to conceive any origin for so strange a device. It is just possible, however, that the sign may have some connection with a tale told of the inhabitants of the town of Coggeshall, about whom so many similar stories are told. One fine night, so says the tale, certain of the natives of that celebrated town observed what they took to be a fine round cheese floating on the surface of a pond. Thereupon, it is further stated, they procured rakes and endeavoured to draw the supposed cheese to land. Nor did they discover, until they had been some time so engaged, that their cheese was merely the reflection of the moon in the water! The SUN is met with twelve times and the RISING SUN nine times. The use of the sun as a sign is very ancient, both in England and on the Continent. A rising sun formed one of the badges of Edward III., and shining suns were used as badges by several other English sovereigns. A sun also forms a prominent charge in the arms of the Distillers' Company. The *Sun in Splendour*, used as a badge by Richard II., is here shown. The engraving is taken from an illuminated manuscript in the Harleian· Collection, wherein the badge is painted on the sail of a ship. Larwood and Hotten suggest that the RISING SUN was, perhaps, adopted as a sign "on account of the favourable omen it presents for a man commencing business." The SUN at *Thaxted seems to have existed since the year 1786 at least, for it is mentioned in the *Chelmsford Chronicle* for January 20th in that year. The SUN Inn at Romford bears the monogram "T.W.L." and the date 1632. The SUN INN in Church Street, Saffron Walden, was once a house of note, but is now a private residence. It was probably built about 1625. The devices, more grotesque than elegant, which adorn its many gables, make it one of the best remaining Essex examples of houses adorned with parge work. In 1646, when it was probably the chief inn in the town, it lodged no less important an individual than Oliver Cromwell. His portrait, painted on the tiles at the side of a fire-place, was found during some recent restorations, and is now in the Museum. It was, doubtless, covered up at the Restoration.[1]   Until about forty years ago there stood beside the main road to Colchester, just outside the parish of Kelvedon, an inn known as the SUN. It is still a curious old house, worthy of notice from the passer-by, but up to the date named it, and even the furniture it contained, exhibited all the characteristics of a sixteenth century house. Its carved woodwork, however, was sold and afterwards accidentally burned and its furniture scattered. The pictorial sign-board of the RISING SUN at Castle Hedingham is very grotesque. It is here represented

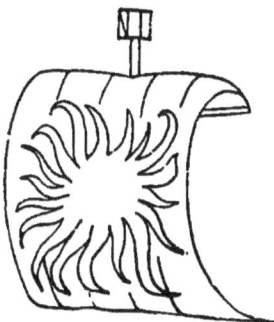

SUN IN SPLENDOUR.
(*Badge of Richard II.*)

---

[1] A view of the house is given in Lord Braybrooke's *History of Audley End and Walden* (p. 153).

within the sign-iron of the BELL at the same place (p. 158).
The RISING SUN at Salcot is many times mentioned in the
Rev. Baring-Gould's *Mehalah*. It is therein (ii. p. 4) thus
described :—" At the end of the village stands a low tavern,
the Rising Sun, a mass of gables. Part of it (the tavern
drinking-room) is only one storey high, but the rest is a
jumble of roofs and lean-to buildings, chimneys and ovens—

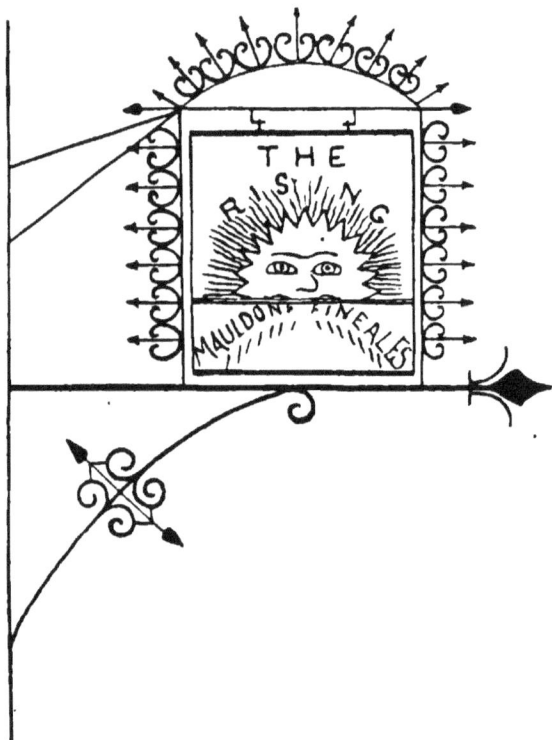

RISING SUN.
(*At Castle Hedingham.*)

a miracle of picturesqueness." As previously stated (pp. 147
and 83) the sun enters into two very absurd combinations, a
SUN AND ANCHOR at Steeple, and a SUN AND WHALEBONE at
Latton. Both of these are, in all probability, impaled signs.
The STAR appears on Essex sign-boards eight times. Its
use is probably due to the fact that in mediæval times

it was the symbol of the Virgin Mary, and that it forms the crest of the Innholders' Company ; but it is very probable that in Essex the sign of the STAR often represents the *mullet argent* which formed one of the chief badges of the De Veres, Earls of Oxford, and also the most prominent charge in the family arms (see p. 70).[1] It was probably first adopted by Robert, the third Earl, who died in 1221. It appears on his seals and on his monument at Hatfield Broad Oak. Thenceforth it was borne by all his descendants. Mr. Elliot, in the interesting article already quoted (p. 70), says that at the Battle of Barnet, in 1471, the defeat of the Lancastrians is attributed to a mistake made by the Earl of Warwick's men ; who, in the morning mist, took the badge of the Earl of Oxford's men for the Yorkist badge of the Sun in Splendour. They accordingly shot at their friends, who, suspecting treachery, cried " Treason ! " and fled from the field. Mr. Elliot adds that "this badge is frequently found on houses and churches in this county and Suffolk." It is in every way probable that it was often put upon the former as a sign. In Heraldry the star, or *étoile*, is represented with six wavy points and not pierced in the centre, as here shown, thus distinguishing it from the mullet, which has five straight points and is usually pierced. The latter is said originally to have represented, not a star, but a spur-rowel. It appears from the parish registers,[2] that there was also a STAR at Grays in 1724. At Ilford there is a coffee-shop with the sign of the MORNING STAR, probably to indicate that it is open early for working men. A beer-house at Witham, however, has the same sign. Mr. King finds in ancient deeds mention of a STAR—either inn, shop, or tenement—at Rochford in 1693. There are now beer-shops of the same name at Ingatestone, Woodham Ferris, and elsewhere, while a NORTHERN STAR exists at

STAR.

MULLET.

---

[1] Quarterly, gules and or ; in the first quarter a mullet argent.
[2] Palin's *Stifford*, p. 82.

Romford. At Brightlingsea there is a STAR OF DENMARK (whatever that might be), and an OLD STAR occurs at Good Easter. Twice, also, as elsewhere mentioned (p. 79), we meet with the STAR AND FLEECE, namely, at Kelvedon and Romford ; while the STAR AND GARTER, representing the Insignia of the Order of the Garter, occurs at Chelmsford and at Newport. An advertisement in the *Chelmsford Chronicle* for February 10, 1786, refers to the STAR at Writtle, and another in the same journal for March 31st following refers to the STAR at Dunmow, at both of which places the sign still exists. The STAR at Kelvedon, perhaps identical with the STAR AND FLEECE now existing there, is mentioned in the issue for the 29th of December in the same year. The *STAR AND ANCHOR which appeared at Colchester sixty years ago was in all probability an impalement. Mr. E. W. Bingham of Castle Hedingham is in possession of documentary evidence showing that during the latter part of last century the present vicarage at that place was known as the BLACK MULLET. It may or may not have been an inn at the time. The sign may have been set up originally as a contrast to the silver mullet of the De Veres. .

CHAPTER X.

MISCELLANEOUS SIGNS.

HE signs which still remain to be treated of defy all efforts to classify them. All classification, indeed, when applied to this subject, is very vague and unsatisfactory. The following will, therefore, be spoken of as "Miscellaneous Signs," and will be taken in any order found most convenient. Those already noticed under other headings will not be referred to again, and many are not of sufficient interest to be worth noticing. The great majority are uninteresting modern vulgarisms, while very few are of heraldic origin.

Many signs of this class are named after places or towns, or after objects of local or general celebrity. Such are the ALBION, the BALMORAL CASTLE, the WINDSOR CASTLE, the WALMER CASTLE, the TROSSACHS HOTEL, the BRIDGE HOTEL, the GIBRALTAR TAVERN, the GRAVING DOCK TAVERN, the HIGHAM HILL TAVERN, the HALLSVILLE TAVERN, the CAMBRIDGE HOTEL, the COMMON GATE, the LONDON TAVERN, the DOCK HOUSE TAVERN, the FOREST GATE, the FOREST GLEN, the TOWN OF AYR, the TRAFALGAR TAVERN, the *WATERLOO TAVERN (at Colchester), the TIDAL BASIN TAVERN, the HALF-WAY TAVERN (at Southchurch), the NORFOLK INN, the GROUND RENT TAVERN, the BRICK AND TILE INN at Copford, two BRITISH INNS, two CANTEENS, two FLAGS, two UNION FLAGS, two FOUNTAINS, the STORES at Willingale Doe (beer-house), the GOLDEN HOUSE at Forest Gate, an IVY CHIMNEYS (beer-house) at Theydon Bois, the RED HOUSE at Ilford, two GUNS, two HOPES (one at

*Southend being at least sixty years old), the IMPERIAL TAVERN, the LOCOMOTIVE, the NEW MILL, the OLD MILL, two PIER HOTELS, two PUNCH BOWLS, the QUART POT, the RED TAPE TAVERN, several ROYAL STANDARDS, the TELEGRAPH, the TEMPLE, the THATCHED HOUSE, the OLD THATCHED HOUSE (a very old inn at Epping), the WARREN INN, the TOLLHOUSE, the WAGGON, and the WAGGON AND HORSES, all of which are probably less than forty years old. It is doubtful whether a single one of these signs could claim an heraldic origin. Most of them lie upon the outskirts of London. There are now four ALMA TAVERNS, though twenty years ago there was but one. The name, of course, commemorates the battle of Alma, but why fresh inns should be thus named so long after the event, is by no means obvious. There is a BOWLING GREEN at Elmstead, near Colchester, and sixty years ago there was another at Dunmow.

The WINDMILL, which is an ancient sign, occurs no less than eight times within the county. In most cases houses have adopted this sign on account of there being a windmill adjacent to them. At Romford there has been for at least sixty years an OLD WINDMILL AND BELLS, which is doubtless an impaled sign.

At Laindon there is a FORTUNE OF WAR, well known as a meet of the Hounds. Larwood and Hotten do not notice the sign, though there are several examples of it in London. The TITLE DEED TAVERN is a small house of recent origin at Buckhurst Hill. Thirty years ago the ground on which it stands was unenclosed forest. At Hornchurch there is an inn with the strange sign of the GOOD INTENT, which is not mentioned by Larwood and Hotten. It was opened as a beershop, some fifty years ago, by the father of the present landlord, who had been so far an unfortunate man. In opening his new house with good intentions for the future, he thus appropriately named it, and his hopes appear to have been realized, as his house still remains. There is a beer-house with the same name at Waltham Holy Cross. At Springfield there is an ENDEAVOUR, which presumably derived its name from some similar circumstance. There are beer-

houses with the motto LIVE AND LET LIVE at Little Canfield, Theydon Bois, and Chadwell Heath. Another at Pitsea
was, within the recollection of Mr. King, thus inscribed :

> " Live and let live
> Whod a though it;"

which was intended to mean " who would have thought it ? "
but the landlord's orthographical knowledge was very imper-
fect. The HAVERING BOWER Inn, situated in Ann Street,
Shadwell, close to Bow Station, is a house connected with,
though not situated in, Essex. Why an inn of this name
should appear thus fifteen miles at least from the place from
which it takes its name, is not very clear.

In the Roman Road at Colchester appears the sign of the
ROMAN URN. One would conclude that the house had been
named after some Roman urn that had been dug up on its
site, did it not figure in the list years ago as the ROMAN
ARMS. Possibly, however, this is a misprint, although the
sign of the ROMAN ARMS does actually occur elsewhere,
namely, in the Roman Road, London, E. Mr. Walford, in
Greater London (vol. i. p. 385), says that there is another
example of the sign of the ROMAN URN just over the county
boundary at Cheshunt, in Hertfordshire. " It is to be seen
embedded in the front of the inn in Crossbrook Street. The
urn was found on the spot many years ago, but its date is far
from certain." Messrs. Larwood and Hotten do not allude
to the sign, which is certainly very uncommon.

One of our very strangest signs—that of the COAL HOLE—
occurs at Leigh. It has only appeared there within the last
few years, and Mr. H. W. King is of opinion that it is
probably named after the once - well - known COAL HOLE
Tavern in the Strand. At the same place another beer-
house is known as the UNITED BRETHREN, probably after a
Friendly Society there ; but their club-house is now the
Crooked Billet.

The sign of the NEW INN, which is the commonest sign in
Devonshire, and occurs no less than one hundred and four
times in that county, is only twice met with in Essex, but

there is also a beer-house so called at Romford. Evidently the Conservative nature of the majority of Essex folk leads them to prefer things *old*, instead of new. At Plaistow there is a GREEN GATE, and forty years since there was a *BLUE POSTS at Witham, in both of which cases the colour of the portals probably served the same office as a sign in distinguishing the house. Neither sign is mentioned in the *History of Sign-boards*, though the former is certainly a century old, as it is mentioned in an advertisement in the *Chelmsford Chronicle* for January 5, 1787, and the latter is referred to in another advertisement on the 23rd of the following month. It was an old house of good standing, as it is also mentioned in the *Very Young Lady's Tour from London to Aldborough and Back* (1804, see p. 37). The writer says :

> " Travellers frequently boast of the charms of an inn,
> But the Blue Posts at Witham's the best I have seen,
> The rooms are so clean, so delicious the diet,
> The landlord so civil, so spruce, and so quiet,
> The servants all round so desirous to please,
> That you find yourself here most completely at ease.
> So we supp'd, and we slept, and we breakfasted too,
> And then bid to Witham a parting adieu."

The house was closed as an inn some time since, and is now a china shop, kept by a prominent Witham teetotal advocate. Its door-posts are still painted blue. Sixty years ago there was another inn of this name at *Colchester. No Essex inn now displays the sign of the GATE, but there are beer-houses of that name at Saffron Walden, Bardfield, and Dagenham. At the two last-named places the houses bear the following very unpoetic couplet :—

> " This Gate hangs high, and hinders none,
> Refresh and pay and travel on."

At Wanstead there is a RED HOUSE, presumably so called from its colour. In 1789 there was an EPPING PLACE Inn at Epping, and a BUSH-FAIR HOUSE at Latton. The ESSEX INN, No 41, Aldgate High Street, London, E., is, without doubt, so named because it forms the stopping-place of many hay-carters and other travellers by road from Essex up to town.

Railways are referred to thirty-one times in all on Essex

sign-boards, although, as might be expected, mention is very rarely made of railways among the signs of forty years ago. Thus we have five examples of the RAILWAY INN, one of the RAILWAY ARMS, two of the RAILWAY BELL, seven of the RAILWAY HOTEL, and sixteen of the RAILWAY TAVERN.

Twenty years ago there was an ABBEY GATE in Stanwell Street, Colchester, doubtless named after the beautiful gateway of St. John's Abbey, which still stands. At the same time there was a BETTING-STAND at Galleywood, where the Chelmsford Races are held, as well as an EXCHANGE INN and a CHELMER INN, both at Heybridge. There is a MARK'S GATE in Markgate, Dagenham ; and a MARSH GATE at Stratford. Eight Essex inns are named after the great GLOBE itself, while the WORLD'S END appears, at last, to have been discovered near Tilbury Fort. This is a very proper name, if, as has been thought, Tilbury is derived from two Saxon words, *Til*, end, and *burgh*, city, *i.e.*, the city at the end of the river road. A beer-house keeper at Paglesham, however, seems also to consider that the WORLD'S END is situated in the vicinity of his house. Probably both are equally right and equally wrong. The GLOBE at *Epping is mentioned in the *Chelmsford Chronicle* for January 13, 1786. At Bocking there is a beer-house known as the DIAL, a device not named by Larwood and Hotten. At the same place there is a PARK END beer-house, and at Felstead another, known as the PYE'S BRIDGE tavern. A beer-house at Chigwell styles itself the RETREAT. At Waltham Abbey is a FLOWER POT. A beerhouse at Inworth is known as the NEW TIMES, while another not far off styles itself the OLD TIMES, probably out of rivalry. At Great Baddow a beer-house appears as the NEW FOUND OUT. At Chelmsford there is a UNITED beer-house, and a CORNUCOPIA at Southend.

No less than forty-two Essex inns display the sign of the BELL. Bells were set up as signs as early as the fourteenth century. The origin of their use in this way is probably due largely to our national fondness for bell-ringing, but partly also to the great veneration in which bells were held in superstitious times. Advertisements which appeared in the

Chelmsford Chronicle refer to the inns with the sign of the BELL at Castle Hedingham, Sible Hedingham, and Purleigh on January 6th, July 21, 1786, and March 2, 1787, respectively. These houses all exist at the present day. The BELL at *Saffron Walden, though it does not now exist, must formerly have been a house of some standing, for it is fairly often referred to in the records of the Corporation. It is mentioned, for instance, in 1642, in 1645, and in 1650. In 1664 3s. was "paid at the Bell when the Quakers were committed," and in 1714 4s. 4d. was "spent at the Bell when Lord Suffolk took the oaths." Tokens are extant, issued by " Will. Mason at the [BELL] in Thaxtead, 1662," though the sign does not now exist there. The BELL at Castle Hedingham, still a first-class hostelry, was a house of considerable note in the old coaching days. It was a stopping-place for the " Old Bury Coach," which passed through the town. The building is ancient and extensive, though now much cut up and divided. The spacious kitchen is roofed with massive timber, black with age. In the large room upstairs have been held for many years the annual meetings of the once-famous Hinckford Hundred Conservative Club. In times past these meetings regularly formed the subject of a leader in the *Times,* and addresses were delivered by Disraeli and other prominent Conservative statesmen, but the club has now lost its old importance. The ornamental sign-iron is represented elsewhere (p. 150). Of the BELL at Leigh, Mr. King writes that he has no particular account, but he believes " it has been an inn for probably a century, and that it was pulled down to make way for the railroad, but rebuilt on part of the same site." The present rectory at West Tilbury was once an inn with the sign of the BELL. The house was built by a speculator about the year 1780, and opened as an hostelry for the accommodation of the gentry that always crowded to the Fort during war time. Six years later, however, it had to be closed, and about the beginning of this century it was purchased for the sum of £700 by the Rev. Sir Adam Gordon, Bart., who then held the living, and presented to the parish as a rectory. A certain number of Bells frequently appear on a sign-board. In such cases the peal of bells in an adjacent belfry is generally alluded to, as may be seen on reference to the Rev. H. A. Cockey's *List of Essex Rings.* In 1662 there was a house with the sign of the ONE BELL at Romford. It is mentioned in the *Account of the Murder of Thomas Kidderminster,* already referred to (p. 56). Taylor also, in 1636, mentions a BELL at Romford, probably the same house. The sign of the FIVE BELLS occurs at Vange and Colne Engaine. At the latter place there are five church bells, but at the former only one, although there may formerly have been more. There was another example of the sign at Bocking forty years ago, when perhaps there were only five bells there. Now, however, there are *six,* and the sign of the SIX BELLS (probably the same house) appears there, as also at Dunmow and Great Waltham. At the former place there are six bells, but at the latter eight. At Boreham a beer-house is known as the SIX BELLS, that being the number at that place. At Mashbury is a cottage still known as the BELLS. In a MS. dated 1761 it is spoken of as the FIVE BELLS, and was probably then an inn with that sign, though no church in the immediate vicinity has that number of bells. The sign of the EIGHT BELLS appears at *Saffron Walden, Great Tey, Belchamp Walter, and Bures Hamlet, at all of which there seem to be peals of eight bells. In addition to these, we have a NEW BELL at Harwich, and two RAILWAY BELLS, one near the station at Maldon, and the other in Trinity Street, Halstead. The bell also enters into numerous combinations, most of which are impalements, and therefore quite meaningless. Thus we have a BELL AND ANCHOR at Canning Town, a COACH AND BELL (a sign not referred to in the *History of Sign-boards*) at Romford, the OLD WINDMILL AND BELLS, also at Romford, and examples of the COCK AND BELL at High Easter, Writtle, and Romford. The latter has apparently been in existence since 1786, as it is mentioned in the *Chelmsford Chronicle* for January 13th in that year. Twenty years ago there was a BELL AND FEATHERS at Stanstead, which seems now to have returned to the use of its former sign, which was a BELL simply (see p. 102). Though the fact is not mentioned by Boyne, tokens with the following inscriptions are extant : " George Perrin at ye Bell in Stanstead. His Half Peny. 1669." The same house and the same landlord are also mentioned in Poor Robin's *Perambulation*, already referred to (p. 66). The writer (one cannot say *poet*) says :

> "From Ugley I next way to Stanstead travell'd,
> Upon a plain highway, well ston'd and gravelled.
> This town of Stanstead, for distinction's sake,
> Doth unto itself the name Montfitchet take,
> From the Montfitchets, once Lords of great fame,
> And who erewhile were owners of the same.
> There at the Bell, at my old friend George Perrin's,
> We drank and tippled like unto a herring ;
> For there is ale and stale beer, strong and mighty,
> Will burn i' the fire like unto *aqua vitæ*,
> And that the reason is, as you may know,
> That this Bell's liquor makes men's clappers go."

In 1868 there was a CLAPPER at Woodham which, perhaps, belonged to one or other of the bells just mentioned.

The CASTLE is a frequent Essex sign, occurring thirteen times in all. It is an ancient sign, which is thought by Larwood and Hotten to have originated in the fact that anciently entertainment was to be had at the castles of the great, as at an inn. In later times the custom arose of naming inns after particular castles, and it is easy to see that the example of the sign now found at Hadleigh, and the two examples now existing at **Colchester, originated in this way. Sixty years ago there was another at *Saffron Walden, which was, of course, named after the old castle there. Not improbably, in some cases, the sign may have been derived from the arms of the Masons' Company.[1] A castle is represented on the seventeenth century token of Thomas Hewes of Castle Hedingham—being, of course, the fine old castle of the De Veres at that place. Mr. King finds mention in some old deeds dated 1693 of the CASTLE AT TRIMME at Rochford in that day. This was probably an inn-sign, but perhaps that of a shop or tenement. It was doubtless so called from the ancient castle of the De Lacys, built in

---

[1] Sable ; on a chevron between three castles argent, a pair of compasses of the first.

1220, at Trim in Ireland, which figured in the Civil War. As this castle does not appear to have had any connection with Essex, the most probable conclusion is that the sign was set up by some one who was present at the surrender of the castle to Cromwell in 1649. The following advertisement appeared in the *Chelmsford Chronicle* on March 2, 1787:

"COCKING. On Friday, March 9th, will be fought a Main of Cocks, at the sign of the CASTLE, Great Oakley, for Two Guineas a Battle, and Five the odds; where the company of all gentlemen and others will be esteemed a favour, by their humble servant William Rayner. The Cocks to be pitted at eleven o'clock, and a good ordinary to be provided at two."

Mr. H. W. King writes:

"The present CASTLE at Hadleigh changed its name (though remaining at the same house) late in the last, or early in the present, century. It was formerly the BLUE BOAR, and old people persistently called it so within my memory, in spite of the change. I have also found evidence of this change in some old Court Rolls. This kind of change is not infrequent. I conceive that the BLUE BOAR may have been the sign of the inn for centuries, but the CASTLE was, I suppose, thought more attractive to the many visitors to the old Castle."

The CHEQUERS is a sign of great interest and antiquity. It is very common in Essex, as it appears no less than twenty times, including one OLD CHEQUERS. It is equally common as a beer-house sign. Robt. Bowyer kept the CHEQUERS at Bardfield in the seventeenth century, as shown by his token, but no house now exists there under that name. Mr. Creed's list (p. 7) shows inns with this sign at Epping, Nazing, Waltham Abbey, High Laver, and Nettleswell in 1789. The CHEQUERS at Roxwell seems to have existed since 1787, as it is referred to in the *Chelmsford Chronicle* for February 2nd in that year. As a sign it is said to be found even among the ruins of Pompeii, and, according to Larwood and Hotten, it "is, perhaps, the most patriarchal of all signs." The same writers say (p. 488) that in England it is "said to represent the coat of arms of the Earls de Warrenne and Surrey, who bore *chequy, or and azure,* and in the reign of Edward IV. possessed the privilege of licensing alehouses." The old money-changers used boards divided up

12

into squares like a modern chess-board, and the sign of the CHEQUERS may have originated, partly, at least, in these " exchequers," as they were called, being hung up outside their places of business. Not improbably the sign also represents the " chequer," or board divided into squares, and still used in some country inns for keeping a tally or record of the amount drunk by each regular customer. As the sign is now painted it is almost as often *lozengy* as *chequy*. In the year 1764, according to an advertisement of that date in the *Chelmsford Chronicle*, the present IPSWICH ARMS at Ingatestone was impaled with a CHEQUERS, forming the IPSWICH ARMS AND CHEQUERS.

The sign of the COACH AND HORSES, which occurs thirteen times in the county, has already been alluded to. As might be expected, it was considerably commoner forty years ago than now. An inn of this name at Chelmsford has a pictorial sign-board, representing a number of gentlemen, in the costume of fifty or sixty years ago, riding on the top of a coach.

Four houses in Essex, situated respectively at Leigh, Barking, Chadwell Heath, and Nazing, now make use of the CROOKED BILLET as their sign. Twenty years ago another did so, and there is still a beer-house so styled at Felstead. There is also an OLD CROOKED BILLET at Walthamstow, and a CROWN AND CROOKED BILLET (doubtless merely an impaled sign) at Woodford Bridge. It is not by any means clear what this sign was derived from. Larwood and Hotten confess

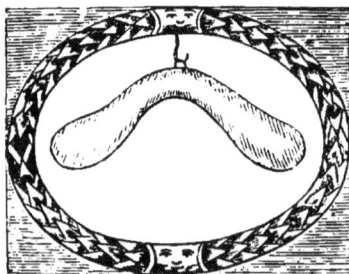

CROOKED BILLET.
(*After Larwood and Hotten.*)

that they " have not been able to discover any likely origin ; it may have been originally a ragged staff, or a pastoral staff. . . . Frequently the sign is represented by an untrimmed stick suspended above the door." Mr. H. W. King writes that the sign existed at Leigh in the earlier part of last century, being

used by a small house which still stands, but is not the
inn now displaying the sign in that town. He says :

"The first mention I find of the existing inn is an admission dated
1765, and referring to a certain tenement adjoining eastward to the lane
leading to the CROOKED BILLET. This previous house of the same name
is a small plaster cottage. It must have been a very mean little public-
house. At some period its sign was transferred to the present house in
the main street, which was formerly a gentleman's residence, and on the
same property as the cottage."

Mr. King adds :

" I incline to think that the CROOKED BILLET was originally a *fess
dancetté* or a *chevron*—more probably the former—and that it is, therefore, an heraldic sign. The sign in this town was originally a pictorial
one, and certainly it rudely represented the former. Now that it is
written a different origin is assigned to it here; but there are so many
others that I rather incline to the heraldic origin. They said here
formerly that faggots were shipped from the wharf opposite the present
house. But so they were from other wharves."

The sign of the CROSS might, with equal probability, be
ascribed either to an ecclesiastical or an heraldic origin : in
the one it is the symbol of Christianity, and in the other it is
a very common ordinary. It came to be used very commonly
as an heraldic charge at the time of the Crusades. The
house with this name at Mistley was, however, probably so
called on account of its being situated at a "four-want-way,"
where two roads cross. There is another example of the sign
at Boxted, and in 1823 there was a RED CROSS at *Colchester.
On the map of the road between London and Harwich, given
in Ogilby's *Itinerarium Angliæ*, published in 1675, a house—
presumably an inn of importance—known as the CROSS AND
HAND, is shown at Marks Tey, and just forty-five miles from
London. Salmon (*History of Essex*, p. 69) quotes an ancient
document, describing the ceremonies connected with the
annual making and presenting of the Wardstaff in Ongar
Hundred, in which another house—probably an inn—with
the sign of "the CROSS WITH A HAND at the three wants
in Fiffield" [Fyfield] is mentioned. In Essex, three or four
roads meeting are spoken of respectively as the three or four
" wants." " The Cross [says Jewitt] whether golden, red,
blue, or otherwise, was formerly a much more common sign

than now." Several other Essex signs are more or less
ecclesiastical. For instance, the *MITRE at Colchester is at
least sixty years old. Very probably it was first so called
after one or other of the several well-known taverns of the
same name which formerly existed in London. Though it
may have been derived from the fact that the Abbot of St.
John's Abbey, at Colchester, was one of the twenty-eight
mitred abbots, and sat in the Upper House of Parliament.
The CARDINAL'S HAT, formerly a not uncommon sign, was
displayed by a house in Bocking forty years since, but has
now disappeared. At Coggeshall, one of the chief inns has
long been known as the *CHAPEL INN. Mr. G. F. Beaumont
has kindly supplied the following information concerning it :

"In the will of Thomas Halle of Coksale, dated Jan. 15th, 1499, and
proved Feb. 5th following, is this Bequest :—' I bequeath towarde the
edifyng and making of a Chapell within the said towne of Coksale XX³,
to be paid when the said Chapell is in werkyng.' In the *Certificate of
Chantry Lands* (1549) is the following under Coggeshall :—' Item, one
olde Chaple in the Street there, with a little Garden, which is worth by
the year 4s.' "

Mr. Beaumont adds : " By deed, dated Oct. 7th, 1588, a
messuage called the old Chapel was conveyed to the fullers
and weavers of Coggeshall. The site of this building, which
was pulled down in 1795, is now open ground, on the west
side of which is the CHAPEL Inn." The sign is probably
unique. The CROSS KEYS, which represent the arms of the
Papal See, appear five times on Essex sign-boards, namely,
at Saffron Walden, *Colchester, White Notley, Dagenham,
and Chadwell St. Mary, while there is a beer-house so
distinguished at North Weald. The Cross Keys have survived the Reformation on account of their appearing also in
the coats of arms of several English sees, namely, York,
Cashel, Exeter, Gloucester, and Peterborough. Three pairs
of keys crossed also form a prominent charge in the arms of
the Fishmongers' Company (see p. 103). Sometimes the
CROSS KEYS was used as a locksmith's sign, as may be
learned from the trade-tokens of the seventeenth century.
Thus THREE KEYS are represented on the farthing of
"Thomas Haven, Locksmith, in Chelmsford, 1669," and

the CROSSED KEYS on that of " Edward Keatchener of Dunmow, Locksmith." The sign of the CROWN is very common in Essex, occurring twenty-eight times altogether. Judging from Mr. Creed's list (p. 7) it was equally common in Essex a century ago. There is also an OLD CROWN at Sandon. As an emblem of Royalty, the badge of several of our Kings and Queens, and as a very frequent heraldic bearing, the Crown is in every way likely to be common. Larwood and Hotten (p. 101) say that it " seems to be one of the oldest of English signs. We read of it as early as 1467, when a certain Walter Walters, who kept the Crown in Cheapside, made an innocent Cockney pun, saying he would make his son heir to the Crown, which so displeased his gracious Majesty, King Edward IV., that he ordered the man to be put to death for high treason." The CROWN at Romford, a once-famous hostelry, built about three centuries ago, was demolished in the spring of 1881, when fine specimens of Tudor work, and some massive beams beautifully carved, were brought to light. It was once of large size, with frontages both to High Street and what is now known as South Street. At the beginning of this century, however, having declined before younger rivals, it was divided into shops. Later a considerable portion was pulled down to make room for a new bank. This demolition, and that of 1881, left nothing standing of the old house except a portion which still remains between the Bank and the WHITE HART Hotel. Mr. King learns from old deeds and from other sources that an inn with the sign of the CROWN existed at Leigh in the time of Queen Elizabeth, when it was known as the " Crown Brewery " or " Crown House," but it does not seem to have retained its existence later than the end of last century or thereabouts. Mr. King believes that this was the inn referred to by " Taylor the Water Poet," in his *Catalogue of Tavernes*, as being kept by a certain James Hare in 1636. No doubt it was an inn also, for, as Mr. King remarks, " all, or nearly all, inns formerly brewed their own beer." He can trace it actually from 1619 and practically from 1570. After it ceased to be an inn it was converted into a private house and bought by a certain Francis Marriage, who after several law-suits resold it. A CROWN also appears on the token, dated 1667, of "Abra. Langley, iunior, of Colchester, Bay-makr." The CROWN at *Billericay (a house not now exist-ing) is referred to in the *Chelmsford Chronicle* for February 17, 1786, and the CROWN at Chesterford is referred to in the same newspaper on the 2nd of March, 1787. Daniel Defoe, in his *Tour through Great Britain*, published in 1724, also mentions the CROWN at Chesterford. Probably this is the house at Little Chesterford still known as the CROWN. The CROWN INN at Brentwood, which was mentioned by Taylor in 1636, was closed many years ago. In 1740, Salmon, who seldom noticed the inns, wrote of it as follows in his *History and Antiquities of Essex* (p. 262) :—

"The Crown Inn here is very ancient, as appears from the buildings of the back part of it. Mr. Symonds in his collection saith he was in-formed from the Master (who had writings in custody to show it) that it had been an Inn 300 years with this sign ; that a family named Salmon held it two hundred years ; and that there had been eighty-nine owners, amongst which [were] an Earl of Oxford and an Earl of Sussex."

The CROWN at Ilford finds mention in the Barking parish register as early as 1595.[1] Fox, in his *Book of Martyrs*, says that George Eagles, who was martyred in 1557, "was carried to the new inn, called by the sign of the CROWN, at Chelmsford" (see p. 136). The sign does not now appear there.

The *Builder* of July 8, 1848, contains an illustration of a fine, old, timber-roofed hall at Saffron Walden. Its interior, we are told, was "so completely hidden by the subdivision of walls and ceilings within it, to adapt it to the necessities of a dwelling-house, that until the demolition of the buildings in the spring of the present year all that could be seen were the carved heads of the ends of the hammer-beams. These heads were beautifully and spiritedly carved, and, indeed, the ornamentation of the entire hall was well and boldly cut. It was of small dimensions. . . . The buildings with which it was connected were old, but no record of the history or occupation of the place is known, except that about two

[1] *Trans. Essex Arch. Soc.*, vol. ii. p. 128.

centuries ago it was an inn, the sign being the IRON CROWN.
The Hall appears to be of the time of Henry VII., judging
from its detail. It may have been the hall of some wealthy
tradesman, for Walden had many rich traders in the olden
time. . . . The ancient hall, and the buildings with which
it was connected, have been pulled down in order to construct
a new market-place. The carved heads from the hammer-
beams (six in all) have been preserved by the Hon. R. C.
Neville (afterwards Lord Braybrooke) in his museum at
Audley End." The origin of this sign is very doubtful.
Larwood and Hotten do not notice it. Goldsmith, in *The
Traveller*, speaks of "Luke's Iron Crown." George and
Luke Doza were two brothers who led a revolt against the
Hungarian nobles at the beginning of the sixteenth century.
They were defeated, captured, and cruelly tortured. George,
not Luke (Goldsmith's memory must have been at fault),
had, among other things, a red-hot iron crown placed on his
head. John of Leyden, an Anabaptist leader, was also
tortured to death in the same way in 1536, but it is difficult
to imagine any connection between these incidents and the
inn at Saffron Walden. What was known as the "Iron
Crown of Lombardy," was not a crown of torture, but one of
the nails used in the Crucifixion, beaten out into a thin rim
of iron, magnificently set in gold and adorned with jewels.
Charlemagne and Napoleon I. were both crowned with it,
but it is hard to see what this had to do with the inn at
Saffron Walden. The sign of the THREE CROWNS occurs
at Rainham, Rowhedge, North Woolwich, and *Halstead.
The sign at the latter place was in existence forty years ago,
at which time another was also in existence. In 1668, Anne
Ellis kept the THREE CROWNS (not necessarily an inn) at
Southminster, as shown by tokens of hers, still extant. An
OLD THREE CROWNS also existed in the county in 1786
according to an advertisement in the *Chelmsford Chronicle* for
the 5th of May in that year. There are several sources from
which the sign of the THREE CROWNS may have been derived.
They might be taken from the arms of the Essex family of
Wiseman (*sable ; a chevron between three crowns argent*), or

from the arms of Chich Priory (*or ; three ducal coronets, gules, two and one*), or from the arms of the Drapers' or the Skinners' Companies, which have already been given. The signs of the CROWN AND THISTLE, the CROWN AND CROOKED BILLET, and the CROWN AND ANCHOR have all been previously noticed. The CROWN AND SCEPTRE, which existed at Chelmsford in 1764, as we learn from an advertisement in the *Chelmsford Chronicle* for that year, was a sign which was doubly emblematic of Royalty. It was, doubtless, merely an impalement. Sixty years ago there was

LEATHER BOTTLE.
(*At Pleshey.*)

a *CROWN AND PUNCH BOWL at Colchester. Doubtless, it too was merely an impaled sign.

Of the sign of the LEATHER BOTTLE we have three examples, situated respectively at Little Laver, Blackmore, and Lexden. The first-named has existed since 1789 at least. There is also a beer-house so called at West Hanningfield. It is an old sign, taken from the "leathern bottels" formerly used to hold liquor, and, as previously mentioned (p. 3), is still to be seen on the cheques and over the door of Messrs. Hoare's Bank in Fleet Street. A beer-shop at Pleshey had on its sign-board until recently a faded, but correct, representation of the LEATHER BOTTLE. Under it, and on another board, is an inscription intimating that George Philpott, the landlord, dispenses "fine Ale's and beer at 4d. per Pott." The sign-board has recently been re-painted, and the bottle is not now so well represented as formerly. Below is a figure of the old board (with the sign-iron of the SIX BELLS at Dunmow (p. 159), its faded "bottle" having been restored from one of several still preserved in the Museum at Saffron Walden. The example at Lexden had, but has not now, a pictorial sign. The house is probably an old one under its present sign, as it appears to have given the name of "Bottle End" to that part of the parish in which it stands—a name it seems to have long had, it being marked on an old map published in 1802. Mr. Thos. B. Daniell writes:

"Not every one has formed an opinion as to what a leather bottle was like. My father—now over eighty years of age—remembers the pictorial sign of the LEATHER BOTTLE, and says that when a boy he distinctly recollects a veritable leather bottle being purchased at a sale by his father. It was a cylindrical belt of black leather, very stout, with two circular ends (also of leather) sewn in, a double thickness of the same material over the bung-hole (which received a cork for stopper) and a short strap to carry it by. Its capacity was about a gallon, and it was nothing like the skin bottles of the East, as some might suppose."

Portions of the Rev. Baring-Gould's *Mehalah* are laid at the LEATHER BOTTLE at Mersey—a fictitious name, unless there is a beer-house there with that sign.

At Bardfield there is a beer-house with the sign of the BOOT, so distinguished unquestionably because the landlord is also a boot and shoe maker, as a partly pictorial board over his door informs passers-by. His pictorial sign-board is here depicted (p. 170) within the old sign-iron of the BELL Inn at the same place. Immediately opposite to the BOOT is another beer-house known as the THREE HORSESHOES, because the landlord also carries on the trade of a farrier and blacksmith. This is not an uncommon way of naming beer-houses and small inns. The *EVENING GUN (which may be regarded as a military sign) appeared at Colchester sixty years ago.

In an agricultural county like Essex it is in no way surprising that as many as eighteen inns should display the sign of the PLOUGH. At Great Chishall a model of a plough, about half the usual size, set up on the top of a pole, serves as a sign. The connection between the PLOUGH AND HARROW, which are combined to form a sign at Leyton, is at once apparent, but not so the connection between the PLOUGH AND SAIL, which is an incomprehensible combination, occurring

BOOT.
(*At Great Bardfield.*)

four times in the county, and already treated of (p. 146). The sign of the HARROW occurs four times, namely, at North Benfleet, Bulphan, *Stratford, and Hornchurch. There is also a beer-house so called at Navestock. It may have had an agricultural origin, but is equally likely to represent, in a corrupted form, the portcullis, which was a favourite badge of Kings Henry VII. and VIII., as already pointed out (p. 24). Another obviously agricultural sign is that of the TWO HURDLES (beer-house) at Beauchamp Roothing. The DRILL HOUSE (beer-shop) at Stanford Rivers, too, is probably another agricultural sign. Doubtless there is, or used to be, near it a house or shed in which a drill was kept. The DRILL INN at Romford is, however, probably a military sign. At Boxted there is a beer-house with the very strange and probably unique sign of the WIG AND FIDGET. Inquiry has elicited the fact that the house was built about forty years ago by a man who was a *Whig* in his political views. His neighbours regarded him also as a "fidgety man;" hence, when the house was opened the people of the parish, having regard to its owner's peculiarities, named it the Whig and Fidget, otherwise the Fidgety Whig. In Stapleford Tawney is a beer-shop with the sign of the MOLE TRAP. It is probably unique. At Loughton is a beer-shop known as the BAG OF NAILS. According to Larwood and Hotten, a bag of nails, with the spikes of the nails sticking through it, was formerly a very common sign, and may be seen on old tokens. The sign seems, in some cases at least, to have been a corruption from the "Bacchanals."

THE PORTCULLIS.
(*Badge of Henry VII.*)

Of the sign of the HOOPS we have two examples, one at Littlebury, the other at *Saffron Walden, while a beer-house at Buttsbury is so designated. Anciently signs were not always painted on a sign-board, as now, but were often carved in wood and suspended within a hoop, from which custom many inns became known as the "Something-on-the-Hoop," and thus the sign of the HOOPS arose.

The WELCH HARP at Waltham Abbey, probably taken from the arms of the Principality of Wales, is presumably the modern form of the HARP, which existed there in 1789 and long after. At the same time, and long after, there was also a HARP at Epping, and twenty years since there was even a JEW'S HARP at Waltham Abbey.

The STILL, which has been used as a sign at Barking for many years, is very appropriate for a spirit-merchant. It occurs on the arms of the Distillers' Company, and is also

depicted on the tokens issued at Thaxted in 1666 by William
Purchas, and on those issued at Witham three years later by
George Robinson. The family of Purchas was well known
in Thaxted two centuries ago. Samuel Purchas, the author
of the quaint, though celebrated, book of travels known as
Purchas, His Pilgrimes, was born there in 1577. Another
member of the family—very possibly a son of the William
mentioned above—came to a very bad end. He murdered
his mother in a fit of drunkenness, and was hung for it about
the year 1635. His " Wofull Lamentation " on the occasion
is to be found in a quaint broadside of about that date
preserved in the celebrated collection known as the *Roxburghe
Ballads* in the British Museum. A LAST occurs on the token
issued at Braintree in 1670 by Thomas Mirrils, who was
doubtless a shoemaker. A PESTLE AND MORTAR are depicted
on the token issued at Felstead in 1669 by Henry Bigg, who
was probably an apothecary. A LIME-KILN is represented
on the halfpenny issued at " Pvrflet Limekill " in 1669 by
Samuel Irons, who was without doubt a lime-burner. THREE
HATS are shown on the halfpenny tokens issued by " Barge
Allen at the [Three Hats] at Stebbing in Essex," and a HAT
on those issued at Stebbing in 1668 by Richard Sayer, who
doubtless kept the same house. The Rev. W. H. Beckett
of Stebbing has inquired of the oldest inhabitants of the
town (two of them being over ninety) without being able to
hear of any tradition as to these signs. Both Allen and
Sayer have been, but are no longer, Stebbing names. The
Two PIPES crossed, which appear on the tokens of Samuel
Leader of Saffron Walden· in 1653, of William Leader of
" Safforn Wallding " in 1668, and of William Martin of
" Brayntry," the THREE TOBACCO-PIPES, which are repre-
sented on the tokens issued in 1666 by " Miles Hacklvitt in
Bilrekey in Essex," and in 1668 by " Thomas Warrin of
Waltham Abby," and the ROLL OF TOBACCO, which is
depicted on the token of " Iohn King, grocer, in Cooldchester,"
were probably, all of them, more or less, tobacconists' signs.
The latter, indeed, is a very common tobacconist's sign at
the present day. A WOODEN PAIL occurs on the token

issued in Moulsham in 1666 by Thomas Joyce, who was perhaps a cooper, and a BUNDLE OF YARN on that of "Iohn Hance of Kelvedon, clothier, 1669." At Epping a large KETTLE, painted red and suspended before a house, indicates that tea and hot water are obtainable within.

There still remain to be noticed several signs which are in use at the present day, though they are not public-house signs. Several such have already been alluded to, as, for instance, the BLACK BOY and the TOBACCO ROLL for a tobacconist, and the BUNCH OF GRAPES for a vintner. The COW or a CALF, too, forms the recognized sign of a dairyman. At Witham a harness-maker displays a harnessed HORSE'S HEAD, life-size, as his sign. Many similar instances of tradesmen, other than publicans, displaying signs indicative of their trades might be named throughout the county. Few public-house signs, however, are more familiar than the THREE GOLDEN BALLS displayed by pawnbrokers. The device is a truly heraldic one, the balls being taken, according to Messrs. Larwood and Hotten (p. 128), from—

"The lower part of the coat of arms of the Dukes of Medici, from whose states, and from Lombardy, nearly all the early bankers came. These capitalists also advanced money on valuable goods, and hence gradually became pawnbrokers. The arms of the Medicis family were *five besants azure*, whence the balls formerly were blue, and only within the last half century have assumed a golden exterior, evidently to gild the pill for those who have dealings with 'my uncle': as for the position in which they are placed, the popular explanation is that there are two chances to one that whatever is brought there will not be redeemed."

According to the same authors (p. 341), the BARBER'S POLE dates from the time when barbers practised phlebotomy: the patient undergoing this operation had to grasp the pole in order to make the blood flow more freely. This use of the pole is illustrated in more than one illuminated MS. As the pole was, of course, liable to be stained with blood, it was painted red: when not in use barbers were in the habit of suspending it outside the door with the white linen swathing-bands twisted round it; this, in later times, gave rise to the pole being painted red and white, or black and white, or even with red, white, and blue lines winding

round it. The POLE was also once a tooth-drawer's sign.
In some cases, too, it is probable that it was intended
punningly to indicate the fact that the barber who displayed
it attended to the needs of peoples' polls. Presumably it
formed the sign of Roger Giles, who is said to have circulated the following amusing advertisement in the neighbourhood of Romford :—

" Roger Giles, Imperceptible Penetrator, Surgin, Paroch Clarke, Etc:,
Etc:, Romford, Essex, hinforms Ladis and Gentlemen that he cuts their
teeth and draws corns without waiten a moment. Blisters on the lowest
turms, and fysicks at a penny a peace. Sells godfathers cordial and
strap-ile, and undertakes to keep any Ladis nales by the year, and so on.
Young Ladis and Gentlemen tort the heart of rideing, and the gramer
language in the natest manner, also grate Kare takein to himprove their
morals and spelling, sarm singing and whisseling. Teaches the jews-arp,
and instructs young Ladis on the gar-tar, and plays the ho-boy. Shotish
poker and all other reels tort at home and abroad. Perfumery in all its
branches. Sells all sorts of stashionary, barth bricks and all other sorts
of sweetmeats, including bees-wax, postage stamps and lusifers : likewise
taturs, roobub, sossages, and other garden stufs : also fruits, such as
hardbake, inguns, toothpicks, ile and tin ware, and other eatables. Sarve,
treacle, winegar, and all other hardware. Further in particular, he has
laid in a stock of tripe, china, epsom salts, lollipops, and other pickles,
such as oysters, apples, and table beer, also silks, satins, and hearth-
stones, and all kinds of kimistry, including waxdolls, rasors, dutch cloks,
and gridirons, and new laid eggs evry day by me Roger Giles. P.S.—I
lectures on joggrefy."

Two very quaint, though modern, tradesmen's signs are
now to be seen in the town of Thaxted, one belonging to a
sweep, the other to a farrier. The former is situated at the
end of the town nearest Dunmow, and consists of a large
picture representing a wide, empty street of houses. A
chimney belonging to one of these houses is belching forth
flame and smoke like a volcano, and a man is just giving the
alarm with much shouting and gesticulation. At the opposite end of the town a farrier displays as his sign a device
rudely cut out of tin or thin sheet-iron, and representing
a horse, held by a boy, and being shod by the man. The
affair evidently once formed a weather-cock, and its appearance in its present position gives it a decidedly comical
aspect.

None of our Essex inns appear to have names quite as

jocose as that of a small public-house to be seen on an unusually long, straight, and uninteresting road near the city of York. It is called the SLIP INN, and probably a good many do " slip in " to relieve the weariness of the way. Nor do our inn-keepers seem able to compete with one at Leigh in Lancashire, who merely places over his door the pithy inscription :—" My sign's in the cellar."

With this we will conclude our examination of " The Trade Signs of Essex." All that it is now possible to do towards bringing to light their much-obscured meanings and original significance, has been done, and it only remains for the author to express the hope that the reader will deem the result satisfactory.

FINIS.

A GLOSSARY OF THE PRINCIPAL HERALDIC TERMS USED IN THE FOREGOING CHAPTERS.

Affrontée, full-faced and fronting.
Argent, silver or white.
Azure, blue.
Badge, see p. 15.
Besant, a Byzantine coin, represented in Heraldry as a round flat piece of gold, without impress.
Blazon, the proper technical description of armorial bearings.
Charge, an heraldic bearing or emblem.
Chequy, a shield divided by horizontal and perpendicular lines into equal square spaces, alternately tinctured.
Chevron, a charge resembling the rafters of a house.
Colours, azure, gules, vert, sable, or purpure.
Couchant, an animal lying down.
Couped, the head or limb of any animal cut off by an even line.
Crest, see p. 15.
Dexter, the right hand.
Escutcheon, a shield of arms.
Escalop, a fan-shell, the pilgrim's badge.
Fess, a broad horizontal bar across the centre of a shield.
Fess dancetté, an indented or zig-zag fess.
Field, the ground or surface of the shield.
Guardant, full-faced.
Gules, red.
Impaled, side by side on the same shield.
Issuant, coming out of.
Lozengy, a shield divided by transverse diagonal lines into equal lozenge-shaped spaces.
Metals, or (gold) and argent (silver).
Or, gold.
Ordinaries, certain common heraldic charges, such as the fess, the pale, the chevron, &c.
Pale, a broad perpendicular bar down the centre of the shield.
Passant, an animal walking past.
Proper, of natural colour.
Quartered, or *quarterly*, a shield divided into four quarters.
Reguardant, looking back.
Sable, black.
Saltire, a broad cross of St. Andrew on the shield.
Sejant, seated.
Sinister, left hand.
Statant, standing.
Supporters, animals which support the shield (see p. 14).
Vert, green.
Volant, flying.

INDEX.

——:o:——

NOTE.—*An asterisk indicates that the sign named is not noted as now occurring or as having occurred, in Essex.*

13

UNWIN BROTHERS, THE GRESHAM PRESS, CHILWORTH AND LONDON.

In the Press, and shortly will be Published, Fcap. 8vo, about 225 pages, semi-flexible scarlet cloth, 2s. 6d. nett.

DURRANT'S
HANDBOOK FOR ESSEX.

A GUIDE TO

The Principal Objects of Interest in each Parish in the County, for the use of Tourists and others,

WITH AN INTRODUCTION,

Treating of its

HISTORY, GEOLOGY, AREA, POPULATION, LITERATURE, ANTI-QUITIES, WORTHIES, NATURAL HISTORY, ETC., ETC.,

BY

MILLER CHRISTY,

Author of "The Trade Signs of Essex," "Our Empire," "The Genus Primula in Essex," "Manitoba Described."

WITH A MAP AND PLANS.

The book will be supplied post free on receipt of 2s. in stamps to sub-scribers who send in their names before Publication to the Publishers, Messrs. E. Durrant and Co., 90, High Street, Chelmsford, who will forward Prospectus and order form on application.

𝕮𝔥𝔢𝔩𝔪𝔰𝔣𝔬𝔯𝔡:

EDMUND DURRANT AND CO.,
90, HIGH STREET.

𝕷𝔬𝔫𝔡𝔬𝔫:

SIMPKIN, MARSHALL, AND CO.,
STATIONERS' HALL COURT, E.C

To be issued by Subscription in the course of 1887.

The Ancient Sepulchral Monuments of Essex.

By FRED. CHANCELLOR, Architect, F.R.I.B.A.

NDER this title it is proposed to publish a Work containing Illustrations, with descriptive text, of the principal Altar Tombs, Effigies, Mural Tablets, and other Memorial Monuments of a date prior to the year 1700, now to be found in the Parish Churches and other places in the County of Essex. The Illustrations will all be drawn to scale from measurements taken on the spot, with Plans, Elevations and Sections, and, where justified by their importance, with details to a larger scale of the Mouldings and Ornaments, and will include at least 150 Plates of Monuments to members of the following Families :—De Vere, Bourchier, Botetort, Pointz, Marney, Fitzwalter, Ratcliffe, De Horkesley, Waldegrave, Mildmay, Smyth, Swynborne, Salberghe, Wiseman, Fyndorne, Gilberd, Petre, Cammocke, Hawkwood, Southcotte, Everard, D'Arcy, Cooke, Stanley, Merry, Audley, Deane, Tryon, Sparrowe, Saunders, Harlakenden, Maynard, Guyon, Freshwater, Wentworth, Northwood, Maxey, Rich, Bendish, Capel, Luckyn, Honywood, Carew, Hervey, Conyers, Monox, Trafford, Tyrell, Cutte, Middleton, Salusbury, Bramston, Rudd, Kempe, Berners, Nivell, Montague, Bertie, Hicks, Webbe, Goring, &c., &c.

The Letterpress of about 150 pages will include a description of each Monument, and, when practicable, a short biographical sketch, with the Family History, Heraldry (if any), and other curious information relating to the person or persons to whom the Monument is erected, and any other matter of Architectural or Antiquarian Interest connected therewith.

The Author has been led to undertake this work for the purpose of preserving correct illustrations of the numerous highly interesting Monuments which still remain scattered about the County of Essex in many of the old Churches, and elsewhere. These old Monuments, from the nature of their construction and materials, are necessarily of a perishable character, and, as a matter of fact, we find that many of those which are mentioned by Weever in his "Funeral Monuments" have disappeared altogether ; it is therefore important that an accurate record should be taken of those which still remain without further delay. Many of them, apart from their architectural beauty, are immensely interesting from their historical associations ; it is hoped, therefore, that this work will commend itself to that increasing class who now make Archæology and everything connected therewith a favourite study.

The Volume will be published rather larger than Quarto Imperial, viz., 16 inches by 12 inches, on toned paper. The Illustrations will be Photo lithographed from the original Drawings, and the Letterpress printed in large clear type. The price of the Book to Subscribers will be £3 3s. A limited number of copies will be printed. Immediately after publication the price will be raised to £4 4s.

For Prospectus and order forms apply to the Author, or to Messrs. Edmund Durrant & Co., Publishers, Chelmsford.

To be published by Subscription early in the year 1887.

RAYS OF LIGHT,

FOR SICK AND WEARY ONES.

"Unto you that fear My name shall the Sun of righteousness arise with healing in his wings."—MAL. iv. 2.

I've found a joy in sorrow, A secret balm for pain,	A beautiful to-morrow, Of sunshine after rain.

COMPILED BY EDITH L. WELLS.

With a Preface

BY THE REV. PREBENDARY HUTTON.

ESSRS. EDMUND DURRANT & CO. have the honour to announce that they will publish early in 1887 a devotional book, consisting of portions of Scripture, and suitable Prayers and Hymns very carefully selected from the works of many of our best known authors, both ancient and modern; the work has been compiled with great care by Mrs. H. C. WELLS, of Broomfield Lodge, Chelmsford.

The book will be well printed in clear type, on good paper, and strongly bound, and will comprise about 416 pages.

The price of the book will be 6s., but it will be supplied to subscribers who send in their names to the publishers, Messrs. Edmund Durrant & Co., High Street, Chelmsford, before publication, at 4s. 6d. per copy. *A specimen page and order form will be sent post free on application.* It is earnestly hoped that all who can will subscribe for one or more copies.

Unless liberal support be given it is almost impossible to publish works of this character without pecuniary loss. A limited number of copies only will be printed. Early application is therefore very necessary. Immediately after publication the price will be raised to 6s.

MESSRS. EDMUND DURRANT & Co.'s
Publications.

ROYAL ILLUSTRATED HISTORY OF EASTERN ENGLAND: Civil, Military, Political, and Ecclesiastical, including a Survey of the Eastern Counties, and Memoirs of County Families, and Eminent Men of every period. By A. D. BAYNE, Esq., Author of "A History of Norwich." With many Illustrations. 2 vols., large 8vo, cloth. 21s.

DOMESDAY BOOK RELATING TO ESSEX. Translated by the late T. C. CHISENHALE-MARSH, Esq. 4to, cloth. 21s. net. *Only a few copies unsold.* Scarce.

THE HISTORY OF ROCHFORD HUNDRED, ESSEX. By PHILIP BENTON, Esq. Now Publishing in Parts, 6d. each. Vol. I. 15s. 6d.; Vol. II. 18s. net.

JOHN NOAKES AND MARY STYLES; or, an Essex Calf's Visit to Tiptree Races. A Poem in the Essex Dialect. By the late CHARLES CLARKE, of Totham Hall. With a Glossary and Portrait. 6d.

SERMONS BY THE LATE VEN. ARCHDEACON MILDMAY. With a Preface by the BISHOP OF ST. ALBANS. 3s. 6d.

A WEAK FAITH: How to Strengthen It. By the Rev. H. D. BURTON. 1d. 6s. per 100 net.

THE DOCTRINE OF THE HOLY EUCHARIST. By the Same Author. Price 2d. 12s. per 100 net.

A FIRST CATECHISM OF BOTANY. By JOHN GIBBS, Author of "The Symmetry of Flowers." Second Edition. 6d.
" It deserves success."—*The Educational Times.*
" Mr. Gibbs's book is of very considerable value, and teachers and learners will be glad to have it."—*Literary World.*
" It is done thoroughly."—*The School Guardian.*

THE SYMMETRY OF FLOWERS. By the Same Author. 4d. sewed.

THE TITHE QUESTION: A Discussion of the Ob- jections Made to the Present Tithe Law. By the Rev. S. T. GIBSON, B.D. Second Edition. 6d. sewed.

NOTES ON THE LEADING FACTS OF THE OLD AND NEW TESTAMENT HISTORY. By the Rev. W. J. PACKE, M.A., Vicar of Feering. 6d. sewed.

CONFIRMATION; or, Laying on of Hands upon those that are Baptized. New Edition. 1d. sewed.

DURRANT'S HANDY FARM LABOUR BOOK. New Edition, with Daily Diary (commencing either Monday or Saturday). 3s. 6d. bound.

FORMS AND SERVICES USED IN THE DIOCESE OF ST. ALBANS. Published by Authority. Lists on application.

EDMUND DURRANT & CO., 90, HIGH ST., CHELMSFORD.

www.ingramcontent.com/pod-product-compliance
Lightning Source LLC
Chambersburg PA
CBHW031058280326
41928CB00049B/1084